Global Zero Alert for Nuclear Forces

Brookings Occasional Papers

Global Zero Alert
for Nuclear Forces

BRUCE G. BLAIR

THE BROOKINGS INSTITUTION
Washington, D.C.

Brookings Occasional Papers

THE BROOKINGS INSTITUTION is a private nonprofit organization devoted to research, education, and publication on important issues of domestic and foreign policy. Its principal purpose is to bring knowledge to bear on the major policy problems facing the American people.

On occasion Brookings authors produce research papers that warrant immediate circulation as contributions to the public debate on current issues of national importance. Because of the circumstances of their production, these Occasional Papers are not subjected to all of the formal review procedures established for the Institution's research publications, and they may be revised at a later date. As in all Brookings publications, the judgments, conclusions, and recommendations presented in the papers are solely those of the authors and should not be attributed to the trustees, officers, or other staff members of the Institution.

Acknowledgments

I wish to thnak John Steinbruner, Ivo Daalder, and Fred Iklé for useful comments and suggestions, and James Schneider for editing the paper. I am especially grateful to Henry W. Kendall for planting the idea of zero alert and inspiring its development.

Research for this study was generously supported by the Carnegie Corporation of New York, the W. Alton Jones Foundation, and the John D. and Catherine T. MacArthur Foundation.

For
Henry W. Kendall

FOR MORE THAN FORTY YEARS the towering presence of nuclear forces testified dramatically to the deep political and ideological conflict between the United States and the Soviet Union.[1] Strategic and tactical nuclear weapons were dispersed around the globe, carried by a host of ground, sea, and airborne delivery systems, poised for launch by the thousands on a moment's notice, and loaded with enough explosive power to inflict apocalyptic devastation within an hour of their unleashing.

While these ominous forces evidenced the antagonisms of the cold war, projecting threats of sudden cold-blooded attack, they also embodied the adversaries' commitment to, and faith in, deterrence. The idea of deterrence held that rationally calculating decisionmakers would refrain from striking first if the opponent could retaliate with devastating effect. War was to be prevented by ensuring that the opposing forces each carried a threat of retaliation that was destructive and credible enough to override any potential gain from striking first. To reinforce this point, the defense establishments deployed forces capable of massive retaliation against tens of thousands of enemy targets. They shortened the fuse on the arsenals, providing the capability to launch a retaliatory strike during the minutes between enemy missile liftoff and arrival. They arranged for the quick transfer of nuclear launch authority to alternative commanders if an enemy strike should decapitate the top leadership. In short, the cold war foes pursued maximum deterrence by creating nuclear postures geared to prompt large-scale retaliation.

In all this planning, safety was a secondary consideration. To be sure, the Russian and U.S. strategic organizations had reasons to doubt that they could survive the political repercussions of any major failure of this responsibility, and both grasped the imperative. Much of their mundane

1. In this introductory section the framing of the issues, and not a few of the specific points, draws heavily on John Steinbruner, "Safety First: The Transformation of Nuclear Weapons Operations," paper prepared for the Common Security Forum, October 18, 1993.

activity was directed at safety during peacetime. They strove to operate nuclear forces in a manner that reliably prevented the accidental, inadvertent, or unauthorized detonation of even a single weapon. Nuclear weapons received continous scrutiny, augmented on occasion by high-level special investigations to identify safety hazards and remedies.[2] Both organizations evolved sophisticated weapon design principles and operational procedures to preserve effective control with widespread dispersal of weapons and benefited in that regard from accumulating experience and the process of error correction it allows. On the essential point—nuclear detonation—the record of accomplishment was perfect, and on lesser but still critical points—notably, nuclear accidents resulting in the dispersal of toxic plutonium—the record was nearly perfect.[3]

That deterrence took precedence over safety is nonetheless demonstrable. Regarding the design and daily operation of individual weapons systems, innumerable trade-offs between these objectives existed, and as a rule safety was not the overriding consideration. (A noteworthy exception was the early U.S. retirement of the short-range attack missile carried by strategic bombers even though this action hampered coverage of some strategic targets.[4]) For example, locks that prevented low-level U.S. commanders from firing strategic weapons were not installed on heavy bombers until the early 1970s and on intercontinental ballistic missiles until the late 1970s. They were installed only after determining that they would not impede carrying out the wartime retaliatory mission. They were never installed on ballistic missile submarines because of their alleged potential to jeopardize the ability of submarine crews to carry out authorized launches.[5] Another

2. One of the most recent broad-based investigations of nuclear weapons security and safeguards was conducted during the Bush administration by the Kirkpatrick Commission on Nuclear Fail-Safe.

3. For a fascinating historical account of the safety of U.S. nuclear weapons operations see Scott D. Sagan, The Limits of Safety: Organizations, Accidents, and Nuclear Weapons (Princeton University Press, 1993).

4. Without the SRAM, U.S. bombers were less capable of performing search and destroy missions against mobile Soviet strategic missiles inside Soviet territory. But the capabilities of U.S. bombers with or without SRAM to conduct such operations with any success were questionable, making the decision to retire the missile relatively easy.

5. A thorough and lucid account of the development of the locks and the controversies surrounding their introduction is Peter D. Feaver, Guarding the

example of the priority given deterrence was the decision to allow the use of missile propellants in Trident and MX missiles that are relatively susceptible to accidental detonation and the use of conventional explosives in Trident warheads that are also relatively prone to accidental detonation.[6] Safety requirements were waived for the sake of wartime performance. For Trident the U.S. navy compromised safety in the interests of increasing the missile's range and the size of the area from which they could fire at Soviet targets. This is a typical example of the balance between deterrence and safety at the level of daily operations.

That deterrence was the primary and safety the secondary commitment during the cold war is more obvious at the strategic planning level. If safety had been a governing influence on overall nuclear postures, strategic forces would not have been so numerous, so dispersed, or so geared to rapid use. Postures that worked at cross-purposes with safety in so many dimensions would not have been adopted in the first place. Even more than the peacetime postures, crisis procedures revealed this emphasis on the deterrent mission.

History's abrupt change of course has put these commitments into a new perspective. Dissolving ideological tensions have dissipated what was presumed to be the potential motive for intentional aggression and reduced the perceived urgency of the deterrent mission. The demise of the Soviet empire and the emergence of a fledgling democracy in Russia not only assuaged long-standing suspicion and enmity, but also eviscerated the conventional military threat to Western Europe. The transformation of U.S.-Russian relations eased the requirements of nuclear deterrence and

Guardians: Civilian Control of Nuclear Weapons in the United States (Cornell University Press, 1992). Relevant details for strategic forces are also given in Bruce G. Blair, The Logic of Accidental Nuclear War (Brookings, 1993).

6. For a detailed and rigorous assessment of such safety concerns and for references to recent academic and governmental studies of nuclear warhead safety, see John R. Harvey and Stefan Michalowski, "Nuclear Weapons Safety: The Case of Trident," Science and Global Security, vol. 4, no.3 (1994), pp. 261-337. An important study of the consequences of nuclear weapons accidents that spread plutonium is Steve Fetter and Frank von Hippel, "The Hazard from Plutonium Dispersal by Nuclear-Warhead Accidents," Science and Global Security, vol. 2, no.1 (1990), pp. 21-42. Concerning the uncertain risk that an accident could cause a nuclear detonation as well as plutonium dispersal, see Nuclear Weapons Safety, Committee Print, Panel on Nuclear Weapons Safety of the House Committee on Armed Services, 101 Cong. 2 sess. (Government Printing Office, December 1990).

allowed for large reductions in stockpiles. The former adversaries seized the opportunity: modernization programs were scaled back and the bulk of their nuclear forces, long-range strategic and short-range tactical, slated for deactivation.

The adjustments in response to the reduction of political tension, however, have not fundamentally altered the established practice of deterrence or the inherent danger it represents. Despite the rollback of the nuclear arsenals, nuclear policy and force deployment on both sides remain devoted to servicing deterrence. Deployments continue to play the retrograde role of deterring deliberate attack. The nuclear confrontation is thus being sustained by a dubious rationale that keeps warheads by the thousands ready for retaliatory launch on a moment's notice—hair-trigger postures that undercut safety.

In major respects the nuclear portfolios are actually being enlarged. Russia, for example, dropped nuclear no-first-use policy from its new military doctrine and expanded the role of nuclear forces to compensate for the sharp decline in the strength of its conventional forces. That decline stems not only from internal factors—the dislocation and dismemberment of the Soviet army, pervasive draft evasion, and the virtual collapse of the military economy—but also from the growing technological superiority of Western conventional forces. Russian defense officials believe that the asymmetry of conventional forces favoring the United States increases the importance of projecting nuclear strength.

Yet Russia's confidence in its nuclear capabilities suffers from that very same asymmetry. Officials worry that Russian nuclear forces along with supporting command-control infrastructure are vulnerable to attack by conventional U.S. weapons—U.S. attack submarines conducting antisubmarine warfare against Russian strategic submarines and U.S. aircraft delivering precision-guided munitions against mobile land-based strategic rockets and radio transmitting centers for communicating with submarines. They also apprehend a growing vulnerability of their strategic forces to U.S. nuclear attack. In any case, Russia is not eager to reduce the profile of nuclear weapons or abandon active alert practices in the face of declining military strength relative not only to the United States but also to China.

The United States appears no less reluctant to further lower its nuclear profile, despite the evaporation of the primary threat justifying nuclear vigilance during the cold war: Soviet invasion of Western Europe. The United States now projects conventional superiority over all prospective adversaries and thus can rely more on conventional and less on nuclear forces. Accordingly, further reciprocal nuclear arms reductions would be beneficial. Yet the U.S. security establishment seems content with the numbers allowed under the START II Treaty and shows little interest in another round of reductions.

The primary reason given for this reluctance is that Russia may revert to authoritarian rule and revive nuclear hostility toward the West.[7] Despite the grim outlook for the rejuvenation of Russia's economy and the projected steep decline in its defense spending for the next decade or more, uncertainty about the Kremlin's attitudes toward the outside world has assumed critical importance in U.S. estimations of the future nuclear threat and in planning its nuclear posture through at least 2005. The Pentagon strongly supports the traditional U.S. strategic mission as an insurance policy. As the defense secretary said in the 1994 annual Defense Department report, "these Cold War tools of nuclear deterrence remain necessary to hedge against a resurgent Russian threat."[8]

While touting old-style deterrence as a hedge against Russia's uncertain future, U.S. nuclear planners also envisage new missions tied loosely to contingencies in the third world. Although counterproliferation policy in the Pentagon envisions the use of conventional weapons primarily in dealing with weapons of mass destruction brandished by third world states, U.S. nuclear forces will doubtless play a major retaliatory and deterrent role.[9] The U.S. Air Force has begun the laborious

---

7. The threat of a militaristic and imperialist Russia hostile to the West emerging in place of a democratic and friendly Russia during the turbulent transition that is under way has been a key theme of the new U.S. secretary of defense, William J. Perry. See, for example, "U.S. to Russia: A Tougher Tone and a Shifting Glance," New York Times, March 21, 1994, p. A9.

8. Department of Defense, *1994 Annual Report* (1994), p. 59.

9. For a discussion of the role of nuclear weapons in dealing with threats from these states, see the Department of Defense *1994 Annual Report*. It argues that "consideration must be given as to whether and how U.S. nuclear weapons and nuclear posture can play a role in deterring the acquisition or use of nuclear weapons or other nations. These questions are even more urgent when one considers the potential for sub-state factions or terrorists to come into the possession of nuclear weapons" (p. 61). It also notes that chemical and biological weapons pose similiar questions: "Since the United States has forsworn chemical and biological weapons,

task of identifying targets in third world nations developing weapons of mass destruction—chemical, biological, and nuclear. (This is not an altogether novel activity in that some third world facilities in this category—for example, Iranian sites—had previously been included in the strategic target list.)[10] And the U.S. Strategic Command has assumed major responsibility for planning for nuclear (using strategic or nonstrategic nuclear weapons) or non-nuclear strikes against this set of targets,[11] whose numbers could easily reach many hundreds and might

the role of U.S. nuclear forces in deterring or responding to such non-nuclear threats must be considered" (p. 61). Another pertinent official source is the U.S. Joint Chiefs of Staff, whose *Doctrine for Joint Nuclear Operations,* joint pub. 3-12 (April 1993), defines a U.S. nuclear retaliatory mission to deal with the use of all types of weapons of mass destruction: "the fundamental purpose of U.S. nuclear forces is to deter the use of weapons of mass destruction, particularly nuclear weapons.... Deterrence of the employment of enemy WMD, whether it be nuclear, biological, or chemical, requires that the enemy leadership believes the United States has both the ability and will to respond promptly and with selective responses that are credible (commensurate with the scale or scope of enemy attacks and the nature of US interests at stake) and militarily effective."

10. Such targets could be assigned to U.S. strategic forces on daily alert, though these forces mainly belong to the strategic reserve force to be employed after a nuclear exchange with Russia. See the discussion in footnote 14. Under this plan, Iran has been targeted since before the fall of the Berlin Wall. For a recent discussion of current worst-case estimates of Iran's nuclear weapons program, see Chris Hedges, "Iran May Be Able To Build an Atomic Bomb in 5 Years, U.S. and Israeli Officials Fear," *New York Times,* January 5, 1995, p. A10. The Israeli prime minister estimates that Iran could develop a nuclear weapon within seven to fifteen years, an estimate considered reasonable by U.S. Defense Secretary William J. Perry, who nonetheless cautions that Iran might find ways to shorten the time. See Mary Curtius, "U.S. Role on Golan Heights Would Be Limited," *Los Angeles Times* (Washington edition), January 10, 1995, p. 2.

11. The former commander in chief of the Strategic Command, General Lee Butler, is said to have recommended in 1993 that his command assume the lead in target planning against weapons of mass destruction in all potential enemy nations. He argued that the Strategic Command possessed unique intelligence and target planning capabilities to provide the president with either conventional or nuclear targeting options on short notice, whether or not the target had been previously located. The commanders in chief who would normally be assigned such missions— for instance, the Europe or Korea commanders—might take weeks to devise such options, according to some estimates. These two regional commanders in particular objected to Butler's proposal, however, leaving the responsibilities for target planning unresolved. Butler's successor, Admiral Henry Chiles, took responsibility

approach a thousand.[12]

China also figures prominently in the global strategic balance as it modernizes its ballistic missile forces. China may ultimately project a greater nuclear threat at the United States.[13] Any significant increase may well prompt a review of U.S. nuclear planning, particularly the decision implemented in the early 1980s to remove China from the U.S. strategic war plan.[14]

---

for global planning of nonstrategic nuclear weapons (such as tactical aircraft with gravity bombs and attack submarines with Tomahawk cruise missiles) in late 1994. The regional commanders, however, apparently continue to balk at the idea of the Strategic Command's planning strikes by conventional weapons. See Elaine M. Grossman, "Korea, Europe CINCs Object to StratCom Bid for Global Planning Role," *Inside the Air Force,* vol. 6 (March 18, 1994), pp. 1, 11-12; and "Stratcom Offers to Play Role in Counterproliferation Target Planning," *Inside the Pentagon,* vol. 10 (December 15, 1994), pp. 1, 6-8.

Under the old division of labor, the Strategic Command supported the theater commanders in planning for regional nuclear strikes by creating selected attack options (SAOs) for implementation by strategic nuclear forces when tasked by the theater commanders' operational plans (theater nuclear options). The single integrated operational plan built by the Strategic Command could thus include SAOs in addition to major attack options and limited attack options. Under the new arrangements, the Strategic Command apparently assumes primary responsibility for building SAO-like options consisting of strategic and nonstrategic nuclear forces. As a rule, options in the standing SIOP are exclusively focused on the former Soviet Union. Using new means of adaptive planning, however, Strategic Command can quickly execute selected attack options or limited attack options aimed at regions outside the former Soviet Union.

12. These estimates assume a minimum of twenty targets for each potential adversary with a chemical, biological, or nuclear program. The number of targets could be many times higher for some countries, and if delivery systems and their logistical and command-control infrastructure are targeted, could easily reach one hundred in each. The aggregate number of targets for all major potential third-world adversaries could exceed a thousand.

13. The status of Chinese nuclear modernization programs is not clear but reportedly features a new mobile ICBM modeled after Russia's SS-25 missile. See Jim Mann, "China Upgrading Nuclear Arms, Experts Say," *Los Angeles Times,* November 9, 1993, p. 2C; Martin Sieff, "Missile Buildup in China Could Threaten U.S.," *Washington Times,* November 12, 1993, p. 16; Jonathan D. Pollack, "The Future of China's Nuclear Weapons Policy," and Litai Xue, "Evolution of China's Nuclear Strategy," in John C. Hopkins and Weixing Hu, eds., *Strategic Views from the Second Tier: The Nuclear Weapons Policies of France, Britain, and China* (University of California Institute on Global Conflict and Cooperation, 1994).

14. The authors of the Pentagon's nuclear posture review completed in September

All these factors work to preserve the nuclear superpowers' traditional deterrent missions and hair-trigger readiness that undercut safety. Other charter nuclear states are no less disposed to invoke deterrence to justify aggressive alert operations. Britain and France seem committed to maintain a significant portion of their nuclear forces on active alert, while China's extensive program of strategic modernization could bring its ballistic missile forces to a comparable level of combat readiness.[15]

Other countries appear to be heading down the same path. In spite of

1994 considered restoring China to the single integrated operating plan (SIOP), and some influential members of the working group advocated this step. The idea was ultimately rejected, however, leaving China as the prime target set in the strategic reserve force. This reserve force can cover nearly 1,000 targets in China, Iran, and elsewhere (for example, nuclear targets in North Korea, Iraq, and Libya) that would be potential wartime adversaries in the aftermath of a nuclear exchange between the United States and Russia. The original idea was to ensure that no nuclear power could coerce the United States following a large-scale nuclear war with Russia. The strategic reserve force was thus created for use after a nuclear war with Russia. Most of the alert weapons assigned to the force are simultaneously committed to the SIOP; hence their primary targets lie mainly in Russia. Their availability in the aftermath of a U.S.-Russian nuclear exchange thus depends on whether the exchange is kept limited (less than all-out).

These reserve weapons could nonetheless be quickly assigned targets and launched against third world facilities irrespective of the Russian context. That is to say, they could be fired with little advance preparation if the national command authorities order it. Preexisting limited attack options, selected attack options, or other options to deal swiftly with third world challenges can be implemented in a matter of hours (compared to a few minutes for preexisting SIOP options).

15. Russia has been materially assisting China by selling it critical missile technology. The transfers include missile safeguards known as blocking devices, facilitating Chinese efforts to increase the combat readiness of nuclear missiles. (At China's request, the United States may provide related safeguards technology.) Such assistance seems incongruent with the widespread belief that the latest Russian military doctrine has dropped the no-first-use pledge because of the country's growing reliance on nuclear weapons to back up its weakened conventional army and particularly to shore up its defense against Chinese conventional forces. It stands to reason that Russia's conventional plight vis-á-vis China would motivate Moscow's nuclear planners to refine their war plan for China (known as Barrier) to permit a growing range of limited nuclear options. By similiar logic, Russia's security interest lies in keeping Chinese nuclear forces technologically undeveloped, not in assisting China to modernize its nuclear forces, even if the thrust of Chinese modernization is to redress a strategic imbalance with the United States. It would appear that Russia's economic interests held sway over these considerations.

strenuous international efforts to deny membership in the nuclear club, de facto and aspiring members not only have nuclear weapons programs but also surely have plans if not current capabilities for weaponization (plans for mating nuclear warheads with dispersed delivery vehicles capable of rapid employment). Intentions and technical progress are difficult to gauge, but the picture is clear enough and does not bode well.

The proliferation of advanced aircraft and ballistic missiles with increasing range and accuracy certainly expand the delivery options. It is reasonable to expect that emerging nuclear states will in the name of deterrence equip, or prepare to equip on short notice, such delivery systems with nuclear weapons from their stockpiles.[16] Whether they actually do so, the fact that the United States, Russia, Great Britain, and France have preserved rapid reaction postures sets an international standard that encourages emulation. Moreover, if the history of the nuclear superpowers is a reliable guide and the classical dilemmas of nuclear security come to bear as strongly on regional dynamics, regional rivals will be induced to shorten the reaction time of their arsenals. In the absence of effective international constraints, the standards for daily combat readiness seem destined to rise.

The obvious agenda should now include provisions to make operational safety the primary consideration. Not only is deterring a deliberate nuclear attack a less demanding problem, but ensuring safety has become more demanding. The disintegration of the former Soviet Union and the dangers emerging from the attendant turmoil—unauthorized, accidental, and inadvertent use of nuclear weapons, and nuclear smuggling—drive home the point that a breakdown of control has replaced a breakdown of deterrence as the basic problem of nuclear security. The specter of nuclear anarchy in the former Soviet Union (FSU) indeed animates U.S. policy toward Russia. U.S. support for the Yeltsin government and Russia's fledgling democratic institutions stems largely from this fear.

Concern about weaknesses in nuclear control, moreover, is not confined to a focus on the FSU. The aspiring nuclear-weapon states also face problems of control, mainly because they lack sophisticated systems for safely managing their arsenals. Although deliberate nuclear aggression

16. India, for example, has tried, so far unsuccessfully, to acquire missile safeguards technology from Russia to allay the concerns of Indian political officials that weaponization of missiles could erode tight central control over their use.

growing out of regional tensions in South Asia, the Korean peninsula, and the Middle East, as well as the Crimea and other potential hot spots around the borders of the former Soviet Union is imaginable, the specter of a catastrophic failure of nuclear command and control looms even larger.

Viewing safety as the paramount goal of nuclear security policy argues for considering basic changes in the operational stance of the nuclear forces. It is particularly evident that their high combat readiness severely undermines safety. Operational safety would be improved were the major defense establishments to lower their alert levels and coax the rest of the world to follow suit.

Maximum safety would be achieved by taking all nuclear weapons off alert, that is, adopting a stance of zero alert in which no weapons are poised for immediate launch.[17] Besides creating a strict international standard of safety for daily alert practices, the universal adoption of zero alert would relieve nuclear tensions between states by removing the threat of a sudden deliberate attack. Certainly, a surprise or short-notice nuclear strike by any of the major nuclear powers is currently implausible. But because all of them except China can, technically speaking, mount one with ease, the strategic nuclear forces of most countries, particularly those of the United States and Russia, maintain a daily posture of rapid reaction to deter it. A remote, hypothetical scenario thus induces alert operations that feed on themselves. Although designed only to deter, the operations confer the ability either to strike back in retaliation or to initiate a sudden attack. The opposing forces create and perpetuate the very threat they seek to thwart, a dynamic that defies regulation even as the cold war winds down. Dampening the interaction by lowering the alert levels requires more multilateral coordination and cooperation than presently exists.

Removing all nuclear weapons from active alert status and establishing international monitoring of the arrangement would severely constrain capabilities for launching a surprise strategic attack. The arrangement would expose the initial preparations for an attack, allow for counterbalancing responses, and thereby deny a decisive preemptive

17. For a related argument advocating the through dealerting of nuclear forces in South Asia, see the creative proposal by George Perkovich, "A Nuclear Third Way in South Asia," *Foreign Policy,* no. 9 (Summer 1993) pp. 85-104.

advantage to any side contemplating redeployment and sneak attack.

In short, zero alert would eliminate the technical pretext for sustaining tense nuclear vigils in the post–cold war era. Besides improving safety, it would relax the nuclear stances, bringing them into harmony with political relations.

The development of this idea or other major operational adjustments must be initiated in broad public discussion. The bureaucracies that evolved the standard practices of deterrence cannot be expected to make safety their primary commitment and deterrence their secondary commitment or to initiate a change as radical as zero alert.[18]

Given the emphasis on deterrence universally ingrained in security policy, typical arms negotiations have little scope for constraining aggressive alert practices. Even with the low ceilings on strategic nuclear arsenals imposed by START II that are to be reached at the turn of the century, the nuclear superpowers could still keep thousands of warheads poised for immediate release. The nuclear control systems that regulate force operations are still peripheral to mainstream arms control notwithstanding two unusual agreements: the 1991 unilateral initiatives removing large numbers U.S. and Soviet nuclear forces from alert, and the 1994 U.S.-Russian agreement not to aim strategic missiles at each other. A simple extrapolation of trends in arms control would project diminishing numbers of weapons but no slowing of their reaction time. The last weapon in the arsenal would still be cocked on hair-trigger alert.

Unless otherwise instructed, the defense bureaucracies and nuclear combat commands will undoubtedly perpetuate the view that deterrence hinges on a posture of rapid reaction. This commitment would not readily yield to the imperative of safety even if zero alert would eliminate the danger of "loose nukes" in the former Soviet Union and elsewhere.

The U.S. defense establishment does acknowledge that nuclear anarchy rather than a failure of deterrence is the most immediate and direct nuclear threat. Recognizing the unstable and transitional character of the Russian political center, the Pentagon has quietly initiated extensive military-to-military contacts to nurture durable cooperation between the U.S. and Russian military establishments. It has also conducted exercises to

---

18. An excellent statement of the principles for effecting this course is found in Fred C. Ikle and Sergei A. Karagonov, *Harmonizing the Evolution of U.S. and Russian Defense Policies* (Center for Strategic and International Studies, 1993).

practice U.S. responses to nuclear anarchy in Russia, including scenarios that feature illicit strategic strikes by Russian commanders. Furthermore, U.S. strategic war planners have worked on options that would allow selective strikes against breakaway units of the Russian nuclear forces in circumstances in which the employment of U.S. nuclear forces might be judged necessary as a last resort. The Pentagon is also spearheading an effort to promote nuclear dismantlement in the former Soviet Union, an endeavor it portrays as an urgent priority of U.S. national security.

If this policy direction were taken to its logical conclusion, the Pentagon would initiate more extensive operational adjustments designed to ensure the maximum safety of nuclear weapons in the FSU and elsewhere. Some variant of zero alert along with other innovative changes in operations would be pursued. That deterring Russian nuclear aggression is still the overriding commitment reveals a strong natural bias. The Pentagon magnifies the threat of aggression because deterrence has been internalized as the essence of its mission. In dealing with fundamental trade-offs between improving safety and preserving combat readiness, the demands of deterrence outweigh safety considerations. Worst-case scenarios of deliberate Russian attack overshadow the very real specter of nuclear chaos and loss of control.

The most recent review of the U.S. nuclear policy, the nuclear posture review completed in September 1994, exemplifies this parochial perspective. It advocates aggressive hedging against a turn for the worse in U.S.-Russian relations. It ignores the safety hazards that persist or grow as a result of aggressive hedging. As discussed later, the review, which President Clinton codified as a presidential decision directive, advances a nuclear force structure and operational posture for the United States that will only make it more difficult for Russia to control its nuclear forces safely. Among other effects, the review reinforces Russia's reliance on quick launch. The operational safety of Russia's nuclear posture is deteriorating, and no amelioration of this danger will result from U.S. nuclear planning. On the contrary, U.S. plans will likely induce Russia to run more operational risks to buttress future deterrence than it ran during the cold war.

Broad public discussion is needed to bring the two conceptions of nuclear threat, the danger of nuclear anarchy and the risk of deliberate aggression, into better focus. Loss of control has emerged as a serious concern that warrants radical adjustments to operational practices that will not be made in the absence of a broad consensus. Public discussion should promote the commitment to nuclear safety and to adjustments such as zero alert, which produces the additional benefit of eliminating the possibility of sudden deliberate attack.

Discussion should crystalize the fact that combative daily alert stances designed to deter coldly calculated surprise attack reflect the inertia of the cold war and neglect the real nuclear dangers of the post–cold war era.

In sum, the problem of nuclear security needs to be reframed with safety at the center. This reformulation must consider active alert practices to be inherently dangerous and assign the highest priority to mitigating the dangers. Because safety is becoming a more demanding problem as a result of the disintegration of the former Soviet Union and growing weapons programs in fledgling nuclear states with immature command systems, governments need to confront the problem squarely with a comprehensive remedy that drastically reduces the risk of a catastrophic failure of nuclear control systems. Zero alert satisfies this criterion.

The next section of this paper analyzes specific problems of nuclear command and control in the former Soviet Union with a view to showing how zero alert would alleviate them. Although few people need to be convinced that the safe management of nuclear weapons is difficult in Russia and other former Soviet republics, it is important to understand the potential dysfunctions in detail to appreciate the merits of zero alert. This remedy is a radical change that will not survive the rigors of political scrutiny unless a persuasive case can be made on its behalf.

Having examined the strains on Russian nuclear command and control, the paper turns to how the Pentagon's nuclear policy review only aggravates them, to the detriment of U.S. nuclear security. The final section, "Relaxing the Nuclear Posture," describes the technical and operational aspects of options for Russia and the United States to lower alert thresholds. The aim is to prove the technical feasibility of zero alert. U.S. forces are the focus of analysis, primarily because more reliable data are available, although the safe operation of U.S. as well as Russian nuclear forces is a matter of concern. Indeed, the command-control systems are sufficiently entwined that problems of operational safety affect everyone. Because many of the hazards of nuclear operations stem from both side's excessive reliance on rapid reaction, mutual safety depends in large measure on joint efforts to eliminate this dangerous posture.

The ultimate configuration of the nuclear forces may or may not conform to the dealerting proposals presented later. These ideas hardly exhaust the creative possibilities. The exercise is meant to encourage nuclear establishments to work together on defining the principles of zero alert, dreaming up ideas, and planning the implementation of sound ones.

Of particular importance is devising a zero-alert posture that remains stable even if a crisis dictates the regeneration of some nuclear forces to a state of immediate launch readiness. A party to a zero-alert agreement conceivably would want a nuclear option to react to some emerging threat posed by a new nuclear power. It is also not beyond imagination that a zero-alert agreement might be honored in the breach, and that the aggrieved nation would feel compelled to increase the alert status of its forces. In planning a zero-alert scheme, such extraordinary circumstances need to be anticipated to ensure a stable transition and end state. Stability is thus a prime desideratum for any peacetime posture of zero alert, for redeploying forces during an emergency, and for the resulting crisis posture. The final section of the study applies this criterion of operational stability in evaluating the recommended plan.

The Specter of Nuclear Anarchy in the Former Soviet Union

With cruel irony the geopolitical revolution that dissolved the Soviet empire and defused the confrontation between the nuclear superpowers has also strained Russia's ability to maintain firm control over its far-flung nuclear arsenal. As the nuclear command and control system of the former Soviet Union came under unprecedented stress, projections of an imminent or eventual catastrophic breakdown shaped worldwide public opinion and the security policies of governments around the globe.

Among the forms that nuclear anarchy in the former Soviet Union might take, the following ranked high on most lists: one, the unauthorized use of nuclear weapons by rebellious commanders in the field; two, loss of control caused by political breakdown at the top of the chain of command in Moscow; three, a Ukrainian grab for independent launch control for nuclear weapons stationed on its territory; and four, the leakage of nuclear bombs, fissionable materials, and nuclear expertise onto the global black market.

A preexisting condition is the source of a fifth nuclear danger. The longstanding Soviet practice of maintaining vast and dispersed nuclear forces in a launch-ready configuration poses a danger of inadvertent release of missiles. Launch-on-warning, the dissemination of firing orders after detecting an enemy nuclear missile strike but before the missiles reach their targets, remains a core element of Russian nuclear strategy. This rapid-reaction posture carries a significant risk that nuclear missiles could be fired on the basis of false warning. The breakup of the Soviet Union increased this risk by politically dismembering the missile attack early warning network.[19]

The wisdom of Western policy responses to the dangers depends on the West's ability to distinguish fact from fiction and to guage the relative magnitude of these problems.

Rogue Commanders in the Field

The danger of unauthorized use of strategic forces by local rogue commanders of land-based rockets, submarine missiles, and bombers is less than is commonly alleged. Moscow micromanages the field operations of these forces to such an extent that subordinates far down the chain of command have little discretionary authority, or physical ability, to do anything without explicit permission from the center. There is an old saw that in Soviet society almost everything was forbidden, and what was permitted was compulsory. This stricture has generally gone by the boards, but it still applies to the nuclear forces.

Stringent technical safeguards reinforce the micromanagement. For instance, to fire their weapons, local commanders need unlocking codes held in Moscow by the general staff.[20] Any attempt by a local launch crew

---

19. As of February 1995 the network of the former Soviet Union continued to operate as an intact system with functional radar sensors in Latvia (Skrunda), Ukraine (Mikachevo and Sevastopol), and Azerbaijan (Lyaki) as well as Russia. Plans to modernize the Skrunda radar have been canceled, however.

20. The headquarters of the strategic rocket forces (SRF) at Perkhushkovo can assume custodial responsibility for the unlocking codes and launch authorization codes needed by all three legs of the Russian strategic forces. This headquarters near Moscow is not normally assigned this role, although provisions were made for it after the 1991 coup attempt. Because the general staff, including its chief, was implicated in the coup, the SRF headquarters became the primary executive agent for strategic attack operations. The general staff headquarters was assigned a reserve role. The primary and reserve status of their communications nets were switched accordingly. The SRF commander in chief was given the requisite codes.

to pick the lock of a silo-based missile would be automatically reported to the war rooms of the general staff and the headquarters of the strategic rocket forces, both in Greater Moscow. These central control posts can then send special commands that sever the communications links of the deviant launch center and transfer launch control to neighboring regimental launch posts. If the lock were somehow picked, the general staff could transmit a zero flight command that would restore the blocking function. Missile silos are also rigged with sensors and other devices designed to detect unlawful entry and automatically disable the launching mechanism. If, despite all these safety precautions, a land-based intercontinental missile are fired without proper authorization, rocket guards units are equipped with machine guns to disable it during liftoff.[21]

Technical safeguards are less extensive for ballistic missile submarines because of the crew's autonomy during long combat patrols at sea.[22] The boats do not maintain continuous two-way communications with higher authority, and the general staff cannot continously monitor their status or electronically override the actions of their crews.

This relative freedom of operation during seventy-eight-day cruises raises the possibility of a renegade crew taking matters into its own hands à la The Hunt for Red October. The safety of submarine operations compared with those of other strategic forces clearly depends more heavily on crew loyalty and discipline, even though Russian submarines are equipped with blocking devices of the sort described earlier. The crew

He also was given a so-called nuclear suitcase used for disseminating launch authorization to senior nuclear commanders (a procedure separate from the dissemination of unlock and launch authorization codes to the individual weapons commanders). Those responsibilities were removed within a year, and the general staff reassumed custody of the unlock and launch codes and other paraphenalia.

21. *Current and Projected National Security Threats to the United States and Its Interests Abroad,* Hearing before the Senate Select Committee on Intelligence, 103 Cong. 2 sess. (GPO, 1994), p. 74.

22. Current patrol rates are very low because of materiel and maintenance shortages. The Russians keep only one or two SSBNs at sea on combat patrol at any time, compared to about ten boats just a few years ago. However, additional submarines are on launch-ready alert in port. SSBNs are designed to allow for quick surface launch from pierside (routinely exercised under launch-on-warning time constraints), and historically their crews have spent more alert time in port than at sea. This alert practice obviously reduces crew autonomy and strengthens safeguards.

normally must receive unlocking codes from the general staff (or an alternative high authority) to activate the boat's launch control systems. Still, given available public information, it is impossible to know whether a renegade crew could take advantage of its autonomy and defeat the safeguard. The Soviets imposed additional organizational safeguards on board the vessels to compensate for the potential weakness in the technical safeguards, but their effectiveness also remains open to question.

The weakest technical safeguards are found on the gravity bombs and cruise missiles for strategic bombers. The locks on the bombs are not sophisticated, and the cruise missiles lack adequate technical protection.[23] To compensate, the Russians store these payloads in depots a mile or so from the airstrips and bombers, where special custodial troops of the general staff guard them.[24] In the event of a nuclear crisis the Russians plan to load the payloads onto the bombers, at which point the main safeguard against unauthorized use consists of a blocking device on the bomber (similiar to the coded switch devices on U.S. bombers that require receipt of codes from higher authority to unlock the bomb racks in the bomb bay) that only special codes held by the general staff can remove. A bomber's flight pattern must also conform to preplanned operations prior to weapons release, a criterion enforced electronically by onboard navigation equipment.

Despite these safeguards the Soviets always kept nuclear payloads separate from the bombers during daily operations. With the possible exception of crises, they never put their bombers on strip alert loaded with nuclear weapons.[25] The Russians have upheld this tradition. Also, Presidents

23. According to Russian sources, a captured cruise missile armed with its nuclear payload could be readily launched from a variety of planes and would produce a nuclear detonation.

24. These troops belong to the twelfth Main Directorate of the Defense Ministry and operate under the direction of the general staff. The arrangement is very similiar to the separate custodial chain of command in Europe in which the fifty-ninthth Ordnance Brigade managed U.S. Army tactical nuclear weapons in the theater.

25. Unbeknownst to the West at the time, the Soviet Union raised its nuclear alert level many times during the cold war, including 1960, 1962 (Cuban missile crisis), 1968 (Czech crisis and Soviet invasion), and 1973 (Arab-Israeli war). On some of these occasions, Soviet long-range bombers were alerted along with the strategic rocket forces. See Blair, *Logic of Accidental Nuclear War*, especially pp. 23-26.

Bush and Gorbachev declared in October 1991 that strategic bombers would be taken off alert and their nuclear armaments put in storage. Both nations continue to abide by this zero-alert pledge for bombers.

The safeguards regime for Russian strategic forces is of course far from ironclad. The blocking devices, for example, are really gimmicks designed to buy time. In the event of a serious breach of safeguards in the field, the Russian military establishment would need to dispatch personnel promptly to suppress the disobedience and restore physical control. If social and political circumstances weaken the cohesion of the military, its ability to deal with such violations would obviously be diminished.

Short of an acute domestic crisis that destroys military cohesion, the prospect of an unauthorized attack by strategic forces is so remote as to be negligible. The risk is being unintentionally driven up, however, by a deep-seated bias in U.S. arms control strategy. The American obsession with Soviet counterforce capabilities resulted in Russian reduction of forces that happened to have the strongest safeguards (the silo-based missiles) and in greater Russian reliance on weapons with relatively weaker safeguards—submarines, bombers, and mobile land-based missiles.

Zero alert offers a preventive remedy. The cheapest and most direct approach to reducing the risk of unauthorized launch is to decrease the launch readiness of all missile forces, going so far as to remove warheads or other vital components from missiles and place them in storage. This measure would drive the risk practically to nil for all scenarios except one in which policymakers order nuclear forces to be rearmed in preparation for war.

Political Incoherence at the Apex

At the upper rungs of the command ladder, Russian control of nuclear weapons is threatened by political incoherence in Moscow. To be reliably effective at the top, the control system must meet two conditions so basic

---

Bruce Menning of the U.S. Army Command and General Staff College recently unearthed another alert episode from the general staff archives in Moscow. During the Berlin crisis in 1961 the Soviets raised the nuclear alert level for the strategic rocket forces, long-range bomber forces, air defense forces, and fighter aviation assets of the military districts and groups of forces. This alert ran from October 13 to November 8, 1961. See "The Berlin Crisis from the Perspective of the Soviet General Staff," Ft. Levenworth, Kans.

they are usually taken for granted. First, the civilian leadership must be competent and virtuous. Second, the military must be thoroughly subordinated to civilian authority. Unfortunately, these conditions cannot be taken for granted in Russia today.

Regarding military subordination, there is a lack of clear civilian authority.[26] President Yeltsin has not created new institutions for civilian control to replace the old Communist party apparatus. His authority rests mainly on personal loyalties, leaving him at the mercy of power struggles at the center of the political system that imperil civilian control in an institutional sense and invite the military to intervene in politics. Although the armed forces feel bound by a professionalism that rejects such intervention, this norm is not a sufficient basis for civilian-military relations over the long term.[27] It is inevitably strained by political crises such as the 1991 coup attempt, the constitutional crises of 1993, and the assault on Chechnya. The strain is in fact continual. Declining defense spending in Russia aggravates it. The deputy minister of defense, Andrei Kokoshin, recently warned of the consequences of plans to halve the defense budget: "It's clear we are heading into a situation where we will be losing control over the armed forces.[28]

Within the nuclear chain of command the significance of tenuous civilian-military allegiances is underscored by the fact that although only the president and the defense minister have the right to order nuclear launches, top Russian military leaders have the technical ability to carry them out. The civilian authorities have the right to decide, but the Russian military, like the U.S. military, holds the unlock and authorization codes

26. This paragraph draws heavily on the comments of David Holloway, "One Year after the Collapse of the USSR: A Panel of Specialists," *Post-Soviet Affairs*, vol. 8 (October-December 1992), pp. 318-22. See also Mikhail Tsypkin, "Will the Military Rule Russia?" *Security Studies*, vol. 2 (Autumn 1992), pp. 38-73; John W. R. Lepingwell, "Soviet Civil-Military Relations and the August Coup," *World Politics*, vol. 4 (July 1992); and Stephen M. Meyer, "How the Threat (and the Coup) Collapsed: The Politicization of the Soviet Military," *International Security*, vol. 16 (Winter 1991-92), pp. 5-38.

27. The armed forces assert themselves on matters they feel relate to their professional competence and sphere of interest—housing, troop withdrawals, protection of Russians living in the former Soviet republics, and START ratification—but have carefully avoided crossing the line into Bonapartism.

28. Marcus Warren, "Russia Risks Mutiny over Defense Cuts, Says Minister," *London Daily Telegraph*, March 11, 1994, p. 18.

necessary to launch a strategic attack. As a technical matter the Russian general staff also controls the transfer of nuclear authority to the president's successors and controls the activation and deactivation of the famous nuclear suitcases, though these are little more than symbolic trappings of power. They are technically dispensable to the launch process. They transmit a so-called permission command to the senior nuclear commanders, a command that only authorizes a launch; it is not necessary to physically enable launch.[29] The general staff sends a different message containing different codes—the so-called direct command—that actually authorizes and enables the dispersed forces to fire.

The essential role that key military officers play in the arrangements for nuclear weapons control thus gives them an inherent ability to determine who in fact is in power, at least in terms of who commands the nuclear forces. The military's obedience to legitimate civilian political authority is thus crucial. Anything that undermines this allegiance would threaten the entire control system.

During the 1991 coup this allegience partially broke down. The defense minister, General Dmitriy Yazov, was one of the major conspirators; the chief of the general staff was also implicated. Gorbachev loyalists in the general staff, however, evidently decided against activating the nuclear suitcase held in reserve for Vice President Gennadiy Yanayev (Gorbachev's legal successor, who was illegally declared acting president during the coup). Furthermore, the senior nuclear commanders in the field—the commanders of the strategic rocket forces, navy, and air force—secretly formed a pact to disobey any nuclear orders sent by the coup plotters. They remained loyal to Gorbachev, a political alignment backed up by the technical wherewithal to severely

29. The suitcases are high-technology versions of the presidential identification codes carried by U.S. national command authorities and certain successors. These U.S. codes are not the ones used in launch messages to enable and authorize nuclear strikes by U.S. forces. The permission command issued by the Russian suitcases may be organizationally and even technically essential under certain circumstances for dissemination of launch authorization and enabling codes by the general staff. But there is little doubt that under various conditions the general staff could work around the established safeguards and trigger the launch of strategic forces on its own accord. A later section of this paper, "Russia's Unsafe Strategy of Launch on Warning," discusses these topics in greater detail.

impede if not completely block the dissemination of launch orders from the general staff through the normal channels of communications down the chain of command.[30] This potential insubordination vis-à-vis the coup leadership actually buttressed the checks and balances at the top and strengthened safety.

The abortive coup underscores the other essential precondition for reliable nuclear control: competent leadership. People too often take for granted that top leaders have political aims that coincide with the national security goals of the state, especially when it comes to matters as grave as nuclear security.[31] The matter of devious intrigue in high places and its effects on nuclear control became very serious during the coup. The plotters' political aims clearly diverged from the goals of the state; and in addition they became desperate, exhausted, and sometimes intoxicated. Besides being prone to bad judgment, these self-annointed leaders sowed some confusion within the nuclear chain of command, and de facto nuclear authority partially devolved to military leaders of the general staff and the nuclear branches of the armed forces.

Russian nuclear control remains susceptible to such lapses of competent civilian leadership, a weakness underscored by the alleged frequent inebriation of the top nuclear authority, President Yeltsin. Any

30. The commander in chief of the strategic rocket forces, for example, could send a zero-flight command restoring the blocking function, or a cancel-launch command terminating the launch authorization, on the heels of an order from the general staff to fire. However, the ability to stymie the general staff completely would depend on extraordinary effort by the SRF to sever communications links and disable equipment, an effort that would take many days to complete. The SRF chain of command runs from its main headquarters near Moscow (and alternate command post at Balbanova south of Moscow) through five SRF armies (the forty-third at Vinnitsa, Ukraine, twenty-seventh at Vladimir, thirty-third at Omsk, thirty-first at Orenburg, and fifty-third at Chita) to divisions, regiments, and individual silos or mobile launchers.

31. A rare exception on the U.S. side concerns an episode during the last year of President Nixon's tenure. At the time there was widespread, but unfounded, suspicion that the global nuclear alert declared during the 1973 Arab-Israeli war was meant as much to distract public attention from Watergate as to deter Soviet military intervention in Egypt. A related anecdote has it that Nixon's despair over his impending impeachment drove Defense Secretary James Schlesinger to instruct the Pentagon to contact him before carrying out any unusual orders from the president.

personnel reliability program worthy of the name would prohibit any individual exhibiting such behavior, regardless of rank and position, from participating in nuclear weapons activities.

Russia's failure to thoroughly subordinate the military to civilian authority also makes nuclear control susceptible to lapses of legitimate political control from the center. An internal Russian proposal floated after the coup indicates just how far civilian authority had to go to create institutional safeguards. The idea was to assign representatives of parliament to the war room of the general staff to guard against any mishandling of the nuclear launch codes. Whatever its merit on narrow technical grounds, the idea was overtaken by larger political events. Yeltsin dissolved the parliament and the old constitution, and along with them went his immediate legal successor, Vice President Alexander Rutskoi and another, parliamentary Speaker Ruslan Khasbulatov, two notches down the line of succession. Yeltsin subsequently decreed that Prime Minister Viktor Chernomyrdin would succeed him in the event of his incapacitation, a pronouncement that underscores the dubious legitimacy and inadequate institutionalization of mechanisms for controlling nuclear operations.[32]

The institutional weakness of Russian nuclear control was featured in a U.S. exercise conducted in the spring of 1992 as part of the U.S. continuity-of-government program, specifically the continuity-of-operations project (code named project 908). The script developed for the exercise to test the continuity of U.S. national command authority assumed that then Vice President Rutskoi toppled President Yeltsin in a Moscow coup. (The scenario anticipated the parliamentary revolt led by Rutskoi in the fall of the following year.) In the ensuing realignment of nuclear control, a commander of a division of strategic missiles belonging to the strategic rocket forces, acting under ambiguous authority, ordered the launch of a small contingent of nuclear-armed ICBMs against the United States.

This apparently regiment-sized attack of ten ICBMs triggered a larger response by U.S. strategic forces designed to wipe out the offending Russian division (a typical SRF division consists of about sixty ICBMs). The U.S. political leadership ordered the counterstrike, which neutralized

32. Alexander Rahr, "Chernomyrdin to Assume Presidency in Case Yeltsin Incapacitated," *RFE/RL Daily Report,* no. 190, October 4, 1993.

many but not all of the belligerent commander's reserve forces. The residual Russian missiles were then fired back at the United States. In the end the devastating exchange expended a total of several hundred high-yield nuclear warheads.

Possibilities of this kind underlie the multipronged policy of the U.S. government to prevent and cope with the breakdown of Russian nuclear control. Besides the diplomatic and economic efforts to shore up the Yeltsin government, the United States has earmarked funds to expedite the dismantlement of Russian nuclear forces and initiated extensive military-to-military contacts to foster cooperation. These contacts, particularly at the level of the nuclear commanders in chief (whose pact to resist any nuclear shenanigans that might emanate from the coup plotters set an instructive precedent in 1991), could prove invaluable in light of the political upheaval at the top of the nuclear chain of command. Mutual confidence at this level could help insulate the Russian nuclear forces from sudden political realignments at the apex. U.S. strategic planners have also surely considered developing options for selectively attacking elements of the Russian nuclear forces that spin out of control, like the division of strategic rockets featured in the 1992 U.S. exercise.

Zero alert once again offers a superior preventive remedy for such a possibility. The Russian nuclear chain of command is entwined in such an unstable political process that radical intervention is warranted. A sweeping measure such as zero alert would absorb the massive uncertainty of future Russian politics and civilian-military relations and halt any further erosion of operational safety. Its scope is commensurate with the magnitude of the problem. Put simply, thousands of launch-ready nuclear arms should not be at the fingertips of leaders of a nation tottering on the edge of political, economic, and social collapse. Zero alert is no panacea for preventing the use of nuclear weapons by a deranged leadership, but the delay it imposes might at least give sensible leaders a chance to bring the situation under control in time to avert disaster.

Ukraine's Bid for Nuclear Status

Ukraine is another tottering state with a nuclear arsenal. Fortunately, its leaders do not have their fingers on the nuclear button and almost certainly do not intend to have. After two years of nuclear gamesmanship, Ukraine's president entered into the Trilateral Agreement with Russia and the United States in January 1994 in which Kiev pledged to relinquish all nuclear arms to Russia within three years. Nuclear fuel for Ukranian commercial power reactors and other compensation were promised by the other signatories. In November 1994 Ukraine's parliament voted overwhelmingly to sign the Nuclear Non-Proliferation Treaty in exchange for security assurances and other benefits. Ukraine may retain possession of at least some nuclear weapons until all the promises of the agreement are kept. But no contingency plan or political consensus to seize operational control appears to exist.

Russian-Ukrainian interdependence ameliorates nuclear tension between them. Ukraine's military-industrial establishment is not ideologically anti-Russian and in fact helps maintain Russian nuclear missile forces. This cooperation has been indispensable because each state produces vital parts of almost all missile systems deployed throughout the former Soviet Union. For instance, Ukraine builds the guidance systems for the SS-18 missiles deployed in Russia and Kazakhstan. It also builds the SS-24 missile deployed in Ukraine and Russia, but Russia has the design bureau and supplies the guidance system. Ukraine builds the blocking devices for strategic missiles in the former Soviet Union, but the devices are engineered and put on line by a design bureau based in St. Petersburg.

Russia is nonetheless hedging its bets on future cooperation; for instance, it terminated joint work on the only land-based missile currently under development (the follow-on mobile SS-25). Moscow has also blamed Kiev for difficulties in maintaining missile and warhead safety. But although Ukraine was not blameless, it had not systematically interfered with strategic rocket forces maintenance activity in silos or warhead storage sites. Both nations bear some responsibility for the poor record of maintenance and the attendant safety hazards, Russia for neglecting on-site maintenance and Ukraine for delaying the repatriation of nuclear warheads in need of repair at Russian facilities. As a consequence, there have been credible reports of radiation leakage equivalent to 40 rads an hour at one local storage facility (Permovaisk) brimming over with defective missile warheads. Neglect of the chemical high explosives in warheads has also increased the risk of an accidental conventional explosion that would release toxic plutonium into the environment (a Chernobyl-class catastrophe in Russia's view). Moscow has exaggerated such dangers, however, and played on international fear in order to exert pressure on Ukraine to relinquish its arsenal. The Russain defense minister even threatened to disavow Moscow's responsibility for nuclear safety in Ukraine because of alleged Ukrainian interference with safety programs and maintenance schedules.[33]

Ukraine's renewed pledges of disarmament under the Trilateral Agreement and the Nuclear Non-Proliferation Treaty dramatically improve the prospects for its nuclear cooperation with Russia. An encouraging sign was the transfer in 1994 of 360 SS-19 and SS-24 warheads from Pervomaisk back to Russia.[34] Another is that Ukraine's avowed interest in operational control remains confined to a desire for a technical veto that would physically prevent Russia from unilaterally launching Ukrainian missiles. In talks in late 1991 Marshal Yevgeni Shaposhnikov of the Commonwealth of Independent States pledged to devise such a veto and install it sometime in 1993. The system never materialized, but at least President Kravchuk was no worse off than President Yeltsin, who also lacks a technical veto (over his own military). Because Ukraine actually builds the blocking devices for Russian missiles, the government may well have investigated veto options on its own.

TECHNICAL ASPECTS OF UKRAINE'S NUCLEAR OPTION. Blocking devices unfortunately do more than just prevent unauthorized launches; they are also integral to the launch process. If Kiev decided to pursue its own launch control, it could take a major step toward the goal simply by replacing the Russian-keyed devices with its own. Ukraine would then be able to activate the flight plans on the missiles and fire them at their predesignated targets. Once Ukraine had the devices in hand, it would take only a few weeks to install them.[35]

---

33. According to a Russian military officer familiar with the situation, Defense Minister Pavel Grachev seriously considered cutting the communications links between Moscow and the blocking devices on Ukrainian strategic missiles to force Ukraine to bear responsibility for safety and answer to the international community. Advisers dissuaded him from taking this extreme step. Interview with the author.

34. Another 340 warheads had been removed from their missiles and 40 missiles had been removed from their silos. "Background Briefing," White House, Office of the Press Secretary, December 5, 1994, p. 3. See also Robert Seely, "Perry Visits Ukraine's Deadliest Missile Sites," *Washington Post,* March 23, 1994, p. A24; and the interview with Defense Secretary William Perry in "Gambling on Ex-Soviet States," *USA Today,* March 15, 1994, p. 9.

35. A Russian expert in this particular technology estimates that Ukraine would need at most one or two months to install the devices and upload the software.

Ukraine's ability to fire the missiles, however, assumes that Russia has not stripped the flight plans and targeting information from the missiles, something the SRF maintenance teams could have easily accomplished already.[36] Recent statements by the commander of the strategic rocket force in fact assert that all Russian strategic land-based rockets have been stripped of target data in conjunction with implementing the U.S.-Russian agreement that obliges the parties to stop targeting each other in peacetime.

For Ukraine to seize launch control, local missile crews would have to be unable or unwilling to prevent the substitution of blocking devices and Russia would have to acquiesce to the grab for operational control—major assumptions indeed. With the notable exception of the commander of the Forty-third Strategic Rocket Army (located at Vinnitsa), under which all Ukrainian strategic missiles are subordinated, and the commander of one of the two missile divisions in Ukraine, none or almost none of the SRF officers in Ukraine have renounced their allegiance to Russia, and their willing participation in any Ukrainian takeover seems very unlikely.

If Ukraine were to seek a credible missile deterrent aimed at Russia, it would also face the daunting task of programming new target sets for the missile computers. This would pose extreme difficulty for the Ukrainian-built SS-24 missiles because their guidance systems are made in Russia. Ukraine could perhaps eventually build the guidance system and match it with the blocking devices, but the effort could take more than a year (a very rough estimate).

The implausibility of this course of action is underscored by the fact that all SS-24 missiles have been deactivated as required by the Trilateral Agreement. Furthermore, Ukrainian confidence in its launch capability would depend on flight testing. Ukraine lacks the requisite test facilities, not to mention permission from surrounding countries to fly over their territory. Another impediment is that the configuration of the silo launchers for the SS-24 and SS-19 missiles apparently precludes rotating the missile azimuth to the extent necessary to fire at Russia. Finally, the SS-24 is a solid-fuel missile that cannot be fired for short ranges. The shortest range in

---

36. Russia may also be able to remove this vital data by remote command from the local launch center or higher command posts; the United States can perform this function with an "overwrite" computer command sent by local launch centers in the ICBM fields.

its testing history is about 1,700 miles, which is 1,100 miles greater than the distance to Moscow from the Ukrainian missile fields. The missile could still threaten Russia from Novosibirsk eastward, however.

The ongoing deactivation of SS-19 missiles (forty by the end of September 1994) also constrains the Ukrainian nuclear option. Ukraine builds the SS-19 guidance system and could possibly aim the missiles at Moscow because they were evidently designed for short-range theater missions against Western Europe as well as intercontinental missions against North America. The SS-19 has been routinely tested at ranges just over 600 miles and could be tested over the Black Sea if necessary. But its silo is not configured for firing at Russia, Ukraine does not build the missile itself, and its service life ends in 1998. Ukraine would have to cannibalize the existing inventory of increasingly decrepid missiles to keep diminishing numbers in launch-ready condition.

A Ukrainian nuclear option may be more feasibly based on air-delivered weapons. Their safeguards are more primitive, they require less maintenance (although Ukraine's Bear-H and Blackjack bombers are severely undermaintained), and they can be employed more flexibly. Also, the bombers and cruise missiles have fallen under the operational control of the Ukrainian Air Force, though Kiev reportedly has offered to give the bombers back to Russia in exchange for reducing Ukraine's energy debt.[37] Ukraine's cruise missiles also appear to be disabled. Russia probably removed the targeting tapes from them, and Ukraine lacks the geodetic data needed to produce guidance tapes with the requisite detail of the terrain over which cruise missiles would fly to attack Russia.

The status of the warheads is less clear. It is believed that they were separated from the cruise missiles and placed in depots near the two bomber airstrips, and that Ukrainian conscripts guard the perimeter of the depots. Ukrainian sources say that some of the officers managing the depots have taken oaths to Ukraine but remain operationally subordinate to the Russian general staff. Russian military sources say that Russia has effectively surrendered custody. In any case, Ukraine could readily overrun and capture the payloads there. Unlike the strategic rockets, stolen bomber payloads could be easily and quickly slipped into the countryside and elude recapture by Russia.

---

37. Ustina Markus, "Russia to Buy Ukrainian Bombers," *OMRI Daily Digest,* no. 39, pt. 1, February 23, 1995.

NET ASSESSMENT: UKRAINE STAYS NON-NUCLEAR. A narrow cost-benefit analysis of these nuclear options is very unlikely to encourage nuclear ambition in Ukraine, but such an assessment is not absolutely conclusive. The initial direct costs of cobbling together a deterrent force out of inherited or seizable assets would be relatively small. Ukraine's actual and potential inventory of missiles, aircraft, and nuclear warheads is huge and paid for. Even though the assets are deteriorating and the country can ill-afford to maintain them let alone support the establishment of a new nuclear infrastructure to produce nuclear self-sufficiency, Ukraine has a relatively cheap short-term nuclear option at its disposal.

Part of the appeal of this option is of course its potential to offset the imbalance of conventional military strength favoring Russia.[38] This

---

38. The conventional balance is lopsided in favor of Russia. First, Ukraine's army is malpositioned under Conventional Forces in Europe (CPE) flank limits. Only a small fraction of its treaty-limited tanks, armored combat vehicles, and artillery can be deployed to defend its borders and Crimea against Russian aggression. Although the flank limits also constrain Russia's ability to threaten Ukraine, the net effect is adverse for Ukraine. Since 1991 Russia has built up a force of fifteen ground divisions and thirteen brigades along its previously undefended western borders running from the Northern through the Moscow to the North Caucasus Military District.

Second, the lopsidedness is made worse by Ukraine's miserable operations and maintenance of forces. This is most evident in the Ukrainian air force, which simply does not fly for want of spare parts. The planes are underserviced and the pilots are rusty. Although former Defense Minister Morozov deserves credit for organizing the remnants of the Soviet forces into a coherent and independent force, its combat readiness is poor. Russian combat readiness has also deteriorated sharply, but it is still probably an order of magnitude better than Ukraine's.

Third, the conventional balance of armed forces is skewed in Russia's favor because Ukraine depends heavily on Russia for oil and gas for its military; it seems to have strategic reserves of these materials. It doubtless has plenty of ammunition, but its logistics train for supporting the deployment of forces in wartime has to be extremely short.

Fourth, the large percentage of ethnic Russian officers in the Ukrainian military raises the question of motivation and morale in the event of conflict with Russia. Despite a concerted effort to indoctrinate and convert this corps, its loyalty to Kiev has to be questioned.

Fifth, Ukraine's economy cannot sustain an effective military. The economy's downward spiral bodes ill for building up and modernizing the army in the next decade.

imbalance poses a deep and long-term structural obstacle to denuclearization in Ukraine. It complements the other more immediate security issues that also might inhibit denuclearization, particularly the dispute over which ships in the Black Sea fleet belong to Ukraine and which to Russia and the threat to Ukrainian territorial integrity posed by the Crimean separatist movement backed by Russian nationalists.

These and other sources of Ukrainian insecurity have the potential to unravel the country's commitment to non-nuclear status. Although its parliament's demands for security guarantees from the nuclear powers (except for China) are being met to its satisfaction,[39] Ukraine voted to join the Nuclear Non-Proliferation Treaty on the condition that the nuclear states refrain from using economic coercion such as embargoes or blockades against it. It reserved the right to reconsider its adherence to the treaty if any of the nuclear states exerts economic or military pressure against it, though such a right of withdrawal inheres in the treaty in any case. Ironically, the day before the vote, Russia is said to have announced it would stop supplying nuclear fuel for Ukrainian nuclear power plants until Ukraine joined the treaty.[40]

A pessimistic scenario would thus have Ukraine reneging on its

On the other side of the ledger is Ukraine's huge inventory of weapons inherited from the Soviet Union, the large size of its army (about half a million), the tremendous decline in Russian military strength, and the intrinsic advantage of a defensive instead of offensive strategy. But the net result still strongly favors Russia. These assessments are tricky, but most likely Russia could successfully grab the eastern portion of the country including Crimea, although Ukraine certainly would be able to mount a strong defense of the western portion, given the current weakness of Russia's military.

39. The United States, Russia, France, and Great Britain have given positive and negative security assurances to Ukraine. The positive assurance pledges that they will go to the UN Security Council on behalf of Ukraine if the country is threatened or attacked by a nuclear-armed state. The negative assurance pledges that none of them will use or threaten to use nuclear weapons against Ukraine as long as it remains a non-nuclear party to the treaty and refrains from allying itself with a nuclear state threatening action against a state offering the assurance. Furthermore, President Leonid Kuchma announced that Ukraine had received official confirmation from the United States, Russia, and Great Britain that they would respect Ukraine's independence, sovereignty, and integrity within its existing borders.

40. Doug Clarke and Ustina Markus, "Ukraine Accedes to NPT," *RFE/RL Daily Report,* no. 218, November 17, 1994.

denuclearization commitments if, for instance, Russia coerced it economically or threatened to annex Crimea to protect the interests of ethnic Russian inhabitants. No prognosis is offered here, but Kiev will probably at least prolong denuclearization as long as possible to test the reliability of Russia's commitment to Ukrainian sovereignty. The schedule for warhead withdrawal under the Trilateral Agreement is missing from the public agreement, but the secret withdrawal terms allow Ukraine nearly two more years to eliminate the remaining weapons. Ukraine could receive virtually all the compensation it has been promised and still preserve a nuclear option simply by pulling up short on the last delivery of the last installment of warheads.

Those warheads would be the bomber payloads whose transfer to Russia is reportedly the last to occur under the secret three-year withdrawal schedule. Control over the warheads is tenuous compared with control of the missile warheads, and they offer the cheapest and most versatile nuclear capability. Ukraine might in the end withhold a portion of this inventory and obtain full-fledged nuclear status even after receiving the bulk of the compensation for its nuclear arsenal.

For this deviation it would sacrifice the security reassurances proffered by the other parties and obviously pay a heavy price in other political and economic terms. This end game thus seems unlikely.

Nevertheless, elements in Ukraine continue to support keeping a nuclear option open as long as possible. Former Defense Minister Kostyantyn Morozov, who authored the original draft of Ukrainian military doctrine that rejected nuclear status, has admitted that he tried to keep a nuclear option open. Because this position could still gain momentum in the event of a deterioration in Ukrainian-Russian relations, the United States should at least prepare a contingency plan to deal with it.[41]

The optimistic view sees the Crimean problem, and the vulnerability of Ukraine generally, as motivating Ukraine's accession to the Nuclear Non-Proliferation Treaty to activate the big-power security assurances predicated on such ratification (as stipulated in the Trilateral Agreement). This view also emphasizes the enormous liabilities of nuclear status.

---

41. An element of that plan should anticipate the potential diversion of some bomber payloads and try to head it off by providing technical assistance and economic incentives soon to consolidate the entire inventory at a central depot and place it under joint U.S.-Russian-Ukrainian monitoring.

Pursuing the nuclear option would not only incur severe political and economic costs but might even provoke an aggressive Russian reaction. If Kiev were to renege on its Trilateral Agreement commitments and seek nuclear status after all, Russia might take the drastic step of cutting off oil, gas, timber, or nuclear fuel supplies to coerce Ukraine to surrender the nuclear arms. Its economy paralyzed, Ukraine might well succumb to the pressure. Or it might view the nuclear option as its last desperate hope to preserve its sovereignty. Whether Kiev would be driven to seize operational control and whether this would beget a hostile Russian military response to preserve its nuclear control, are open questions. But in all likelihood a Ukrainian grab for control would trigger a military fight over nuclear weapons custody. An early draft of Russia's new military doctrine appeared to carry exactly this warning by saying that any interference with Russian strategic nuclear command and control would constitute an immediate military threat to Russia.

In sum, Ukraine's alleged drift toward nuclear status has been arrested and, in all likelihood, permanently reversed. In late 1992 a U.S. national intelligence estimate reportedly reflected "a broad consensus among government analysts that Ukraine is now as likely to keep the nuclear weapons as it is to give them up."[42] My view at the time was that the prediction was "debatable and probably wrong. The Ukrainian government—the executive branch and the vast majority of the legislators—still subscribes to its early and bold declaration of intent to become a non-nuclear state."[43] Ukraine's commitment to denuclearization appears even stronger today, though doubts linger that will take another couple of years to dispel.

The nuclear tension between Ukraine and Russia is in effect being defused by a zero-alert remedy. Deactivating missiles and removing warheads is probably further along than commonly believed. Russia has apparently taken all Ukrainian strategic forces out of its war plan, reason enough to have taken all the missile forces off alert. Any efforts at maintaining them probably are devoted more to ensuring a controlled and safe deactivation than to keeping them combat ready.

If the Trilateral Agreement and the Nuclear Non-Proliferation Treaty

42. R. Jeffrey Smith, "Officials See Shift in Ukraine's Nuclear Position," *Washington Post,* December 19, 1992, p. 10.
43. Blair, *Logic of Accidental Nuclear War,* p. 261.

accession unravel—an unlikely prospect—increased pressure on Ukraine to relinquish the arms quickly could be counterproductive. The action might precipitate the disintegration of nuclear command and control in Ukraine as the two main antagonists maneuvered for operational custody. The immediate international goal in these circumstances should be to ensure that the removal of warheads from missiles is completed and that these and all remaining bomber warheads in Ukrainian storage depots are subjected to international monitoring. An international team including Ukrainian, Russian, American, and other inspectors should constantly monitor all the depots. This arrangement would allay the main fears of all three parties. Russia and the United States would be assured that Ukraine would not acquire operational control. Ukraine would derive considerable security assurance from the presence of American personnel at military facilities on its territory. The off-loading of warheads and the American presence would also uphold Ukraine's right to prevent Russia from using nuclear weapons deployed on Ukrainian territory.

Nuclear Leakage

Economic, social, and political conditions within the former Soviet Union seem conducive to nuclear smuggling and an exodus of nuclear expertise to emerging nuclear states. Both the supply and demand pictures portend movement of nuclear materials or brainpower onto the black market and into the hands of terrorists or states such as Iran and Libya.

The seriousness with which the U.S. government takes such possibilities is evident in one nuclear exercise conducted in 1992 as part of U.S. planning for continuity of government. The exercise assumed that Russian nuclear weapons had come into the hands of Libya, which planted them in several major American cities and exploded one in Washington. Such easy access to Russian warheads was of course an artifact of an exercise; its relevance to reality has not been established. So far.

Many thousands of Russian nuclear weapons have been shuttled around in recent years as the weapons were withdrawn from eastern Europe, the former Soviet republics, and Soviet ships. How many thousands is uncertain, as are their current storage locations. The Russians have promised to disclose the size of their nuclear inventory, perhaps at the next U.S.-Russian summit. But until then U.S. estimates of weapons at various field and storage sites rely heavily on indirect evidence, for instance the apparent storage capacity of suspect bunkers detected through surveillance from space. Official U.S. intelligence estimates put the inventory of strategic and nonstrategic nuclear weapons at 30,000, but Russian sources have indicated a much higher number. The highest reported figure was 47,000 as of 1992.[44] Russia has agreed to supply aggregate numbers of nuclear weapons in its stockpile, but at the time of this writing the numbers, particularly of nonstrategic weapons, remained uncertain. In late September 1994 the Pentagon estimated the stockpile of nonstrategic warheads to be between 6,000 and 13,000.[45]

Although the partial consolidation of widely dispersed inventories has surely improved security, the few large military central depots in Russia are probably brimming over with excess inventory, while many smaller, ill-designed facilities are likely trying to handle the overflow. These stockpiles normally are guarded by special security troops of the Ministry of Defense.[46] In addition to these perimeter guards, a separate unit composed of officers of the Twelfth Directorate of the Defense Ministry normally performs custodial responsibilities—weapons control, accounting, and transport. Security for the region would be provided by interior troops of the Eigth Directorate of the Ministry of Interior. Another layer of security would normally consist of personnel from the Third Directorate of the Russian Federal Counterintelligence Service (FSK), formerly the KGB. This special department presumably continues its historical function of conducting counterintelligence operations within the military guard and custodial units that watch over the nuclear stockpiles at military bases. The Third Directorate is itself monitored by the Second Directorate of the FSK, which has overall responsibility for counterintelligence.

Many thousands of weapons have been dismantled and more thousands are slated for disassembly. The Ministry of Atomic Energy (Minatom) is responsible for dismantlement and for a wide range of related activities within the nuclear weapons complex: the production of the fissionable materials for weapons, design of weapons at special laboratories,

44. This figure was given to the author by a Soviet military officer in 1992. According to this source, the inventory peaked at 55,000 about 1985. See Blair, *Logic of Accidental Nuclear War*, pp. 106, 306, 315.

45. Press conference held by Secretary of Defense William J. Perry, September 22, 1994.

46. I am indebted to John Hines for sharing his research findings and insights into Russian nuclear security.

manufacturing of warhead components, storage of plutonium pits and highly enriched uranium removed from weapons during disassembly, and blending down of highly enriched bomb uranium to less rich uranium for use in civilian power reactors.[47] Weapons-grade materials, some of which are processed for purposes other than bombs, are mainly though not exclusively handled at fifteen large warhead production and nuclear fuel processing facilities, and ten research centers, all operated by Minatom, except for the famous Kurchatov Institute in Moscow.[48]

Minatom also bears the major responsibility for security, materials control, and accounting for the weapons and raw nuclear materials in its possession. Physical security at the gate, perimeter, and grounds of the key facilities is provided by troops from the Main Directorate of the Ministry of Interior. Other physical security, accounting functions, and personnel reliability responsibilities are provided by Minatom's First Department. At each Minatom major facility in the nuclear weapons complex, First Department personnel report to the facility's deputy director for security, who is in turn an agent of, and subordinated to, the Sixth Directorate of the FSK. Its mission is to prevent "industrial espionage," and to this end it manages agents working inside the facility. Overlaid on this mission is that of the Second Directorate of the FSK with overall responsibility for counterintelligence operations.

Compared with the weapons at military central depots, the weapons

47. An indispensable source of information about Minatom's nuclear activities, facilities, and estimated nuclear inventories is a report published periodically by the Carnegie Endowment for International Peace and the Monterey Institute of International Studies, *Nuclear Successor States of the Soviet Union*. The latest report is no. 2 (December 1994).

48. Kurchatov, deemed a high-risk facility, became independent of Minatom in 1992. The major Minatom sites that process and possess large quantities of nuclear bomb-grade material and are deemed high-risk facilities are: (1) warhead facilities—assembly and disassembly (Arzamas-16, Sverdlovsk-45) and warhead design (Arzamas-16, Chelyabinsk-70); (2) fuel production and processing facilities (Tomsk-7, Mayak, Krasnoyarsk-26, Sverdlovsk-44, Electrostal, Novosibirsk); and (3) research centers (Institute of Physics at Obninsk, Institute for Atomic Reactors at Dimitrovgrad, Luch Scientific Association at Podolsk, Bochvar Institute at Moscow). Oleg Bukharin, "Cooperation between US and Minatom in the Area of Fissile Material Safeguards," Princeton University, January 27, 1995. Many of these facilities are not involved in making bombs and are outside the nuclear weapons complex.

and weapons-grade nuclear materials handled at Minatom facilities lend themselves more readily to theft and diversion because of their smaller size and the difficult accounting caused by large throughputs of materials and waste streams in a multitude of chemical and physical forms. Compared with weapons stockpiles under military custody, these allow insiders more opportunities to smuggle materials out. Diversion and export of large quantities would be possible if there were collusion among Minatom and FSK security insiders at a given facility.

The dangers of diversion are all the more real because the morale and well-being of nuclear custodians at all levels has deteriorated. In the current economic climate the temptation to sell expertise or stolen nuclear materials for large sums of money is irresistable for some. The decline of discipline, law and order, and central authority, combined with the rise of organized crime and corruption, have weakened the barriers to the smuggling of nuclear contraband. Bureaucratic in-fighting among the Ministries of Defense, Interior, and Atomic Energy; intelligence and police organizations; and a newly formed state Nuclear Oversight Committee (Gosatomnadzor, or GAN) exacerbates the problem.[49]

And the demand for nuclear components and materials has presumably grown in this era of global nuclear proliferation. One can only presume that potential buyers of weapons-grade nuclear materials are plentiful. If intact nuclear weapons could be bought on the black market, aspiring nuclear states could gain instant nuclear status without the cost, time, and trouble of building an indigenous program of weapons development.

HEMORRHAGE OR HYSTERIA? The combination of these factors helps explain the rampant speculation in the press that the former Soviet Union is hemmorhaging nuclear materials. Given current conditions, one can readily accept the sober judgment of a recent report by the National Academy of Sciences that the problem of plutonium storage and disposition in the FSU is a "clear and present danger."[50] And recent

---

49. President Yeltsin created GAN as a federal nuclear regulatory agency responsible for safeguards regulations and inspections with jurisdiction over both Minatom and the Defense Department. Its thirty-person staff, budget, and access to the regulated ministries' operations are woefully inadequate, however.

50. National Academy of Sciences, Committee on International Security and Arms Control, *Management and Disposition of Excess Weapons Plutonium* (Washington: National Academy Press, 1994).

incidents of nuclear smuggling appear to corroborate the more alarmist view that a trickle of illicit trade is already swelling into a flood.[51]

But with rare exceptions, the nuclear weapons complex, as opposed to other sectors of the FSU nuclear infrastructure, does not appear to be implicated in these incidents. Despite the sensational stories, government officials who track such developments have found no evidence of significant diversions of nuclear contraband from the Russian weapons complex.[52] A possible exception concerns a few grams of pure plutonium

51. A good overview and perspective on these incidents is Spurgeon M. Keeny, Jr., "Nuclear Smugglers Spark Worries over Russian Safeguards," *Arms Control Today*, vol. 24 (September 1994), pp. 25, 32. Detailed press reports include William J. Broad, "Russians Suspect 3 Sites as Source of Seized A-Fuel," *New York Times*, August 19, 1994, p. A11; Lee Hockstader, "Russia Announces Probe into Origins of Nuclear Material," *Washington Post*, August 19, 1994, p. A32; Daniel Williams and John F. Harris, "U.S. Uncertain About Origin of Seized Nuclear Material," *Washington Post*, August 18, 1994, p. A28; Steve Coll, "Stolen Plutonium Tied to Arms Labs," *Washington Post,* August 17, 1994, p. A1; William J. Broad, "Experts in U.S. Call Plutonium Not Arms-Level," *New York Times*, August 17, 1994, p. A1; Craig R. Whitney, "Germans Suspect Russian Military in Plutonium Sale," *New York Times*, August 16, 1994, p. A1; Craig R. Whitney, "Germans Seize 3d Atom Sample, Smuggled by Plane from Russia," *New York Times*, August 14, 1994, p. A1; and Craig R. Whitney, "A Second 'Sample' of Atomic Material Found in Germany," *New York Times*, August 12, 1994, p. A1.

52. The director of central intelligence testified in February 1993 that although Russia's ability to maintain control of its nuclear weapons and technologies had been "somewhat weakened," the CIA had detected no "transfers of weapons-grade material in significant quantities. We have no credible reporting that nuclear weapons have left CIS territory, and we do not believe that nuclear weapon design information has been sold or transferred to foreign states." James Woolsey, testimony before the Senate Governmental Affairs Committee, February 24, 1993, p. 4. More recently, an official of the Defense Intelligence Agency reiterated Woolsey's assessment: "we have no convincing evidence ... that any weapon-grade nuclear materials have been sold or transferred to third parties." This official further noted that "while many scientists had emigrated, "very few, if any, have detailed knowledge of nuclear weapons designs." Citing Russian estimates that 2,000 to 3,000 scientists possess such knowledge, the official asserted that these scientists are located in a few institutes where they remain closely monitored by Russian authorities. William Grundmann, statement to the Joint Economic Committee of Congress, July 15, 1994, pp 26-27. Finally, a U.S. intelligence official in conversation with the author reported in February 1995 that all evidence as of then indicated that no nuclear material produced for weapons, or taken from such weapons, had leaked out of the FSU.

seized by German authorities in Tengen in 1994.[53] This material may have been originally produced at one of the two main nuclear weapons design bureaus (the research institute at Arzamas-16) as part of a plutonium enrichment experiment conducted decades ago. Although this is speculative, the plutonium apparently was not produced for nuclear weapons and specimens of it were widely distributed in small allotments to civil and military research facilities throughout the FSU. The Tengen incident presumably began as a theft from one of these facilities, but the origin of the material remains a mystery.

The apparent effectiveness of safeguards on nuclear weapons and their ingredients reflects the high priority of nuclear command and control in the Russian political and military culture. The Soviets went to extraordinary lengths to ensure strict central control over nuclear force deployments, an obsession that ran through the entire weapons cycle from production and assembly to operational deployment to dismantlement. The Russians show no overt signs of relaxing the earlier standards and express confidence in their ability to prevent nuclear smuggling. Sergey Stepashin, director of the FSK, said to Louis J. Freeh, director of the FBI, at a Moscow meeting in July 1994 that Russian weapons remain secure: "Stepashin declared, as the head of the agency responsible for protecting Russia's nuclear arsenals, that he guaranteed the protection of those arsenals. He said that, at present, there is no serious threat of proliferation from Russia to the rest of the world."[54]

The FSK director's assessment appears warranted for nuclear weapons under military control. It is less persuasive for the nuclear weapons complex under Minatom control and questionable for nuclear materials outside the nuclear weapons complex (most but not all of which are also Minatom's responsibility)—that is, nuclear materials usually under Minatom control produced for and by nonweapons activities in the research, commercial power, and military sectors. Minatom control of commercial nuclear fuel or fuel rods for naval reactors, for example, appears lax.

53. This discussion draws heavily on Mark Hibbs, "Plutonium, Politics, and Panic," *Bulletin of the Atomic Scientists*, vol. 50 (November-December 1994), pp. 24-31.

54. "Joint United States Law Enforcement Visit, June 27, 1994, through July 6, 1994," signed by Louis Freeh and others, August 4, 1994.

Looser security within the nonweapons nuclear infrastructure reflects a misconception, widespread in the FSU, that aspiring nuclear states or terrorists would seek only weapons-grade nuclear materials because of the difficulty of making a bomb from the less pure materials that circulate within the nonweapons sectors.[55] Like Japan and some other states, Russia has been slow to recognize the inherent danger posed by reactor-grade plutonium, for example, and by uranium enriched to levels that would, for purposes of building an atomic bomb, be suboptimal. Material that is not weapons grade often is weapons usable in that it could be fashioned into a nuclear bomb, albeit a more unwieldy one with less explosive power.[56]

The nuclear material at most risk falls under this category of weapons usable. The risk derives from its widespread dispersal throughout the FSU—scores of Minatom sites as well as many non-Minatom facilities—and from the relative laxity of safeguards over its disposition. In a rare admission, Russia confirmed one instance of the theft of highly enriched uranium at the Luch plant in Podolsk, which manufactures space-based nuclear reactors. And the largest cache of material smuggled into Germany—hundreds of grams of plutonium containing about 87 percent plutonium 239, which is most suitable for weapons—is suspected of having leaked from Minatom's civilian-oriented nuclear research sector,

55. Weapons-grade nuclear materials refer to highly enriched uranium containing more than 90 percent uranium 235, about fifteen to twenty kilograms of which are usually required to manufacture a nuclear bomb, or plutonium containing about 93 percent plutonium 239 and less than 7 percent plutonium 240, about three to five kilograms of which are usually required to manufacture a nuclear bomb. The plutonium bomb dropped on Nagasaki in 1945 contained about six kilograms and produced an explosive yield of about twenty kilotons. As little as one kilogram of weapons-grade plutonium can apparently be fashioned into a bomb, albeit low yield (approximately one kiloton). Arjun Makhijani and Annie Makhijani, *Fissile Materials in a Glass, Darkly* (Institute for Energy and Environmental Research, 1995), pp. 10, 17, 18, 116.

56. For example, the United States conducted a successful nuclear test using reactor-grade plutonium in 1962. This material typically contains 55 to 60 percent plutonium 239 and at least 19 percent plutonium 240. Similiarly, a nuclear bomb can be manufactured from uranium containing as little as 20 percent uranium 235, though at this level of enrichment the amount of the material required would be about 250 kilograms (compared to 15 to 20 kilograms needed for making a bomb from weapons-grade (more than 90 percent uranium 235) uranium. Makhijani and Makhijani, *Fissile Materials*, pp. 10, 17, 120.

particularly facilities such as the reactor research institute at Dmitrovgrad.[57] The Russian chief of nonproliferation in the Foreign Intelligence Service, however, claims the material did not come from Russia because "plutonium of such an isotope composition has never been produced in Russia."[58]

Nevertheless, safeguards at Dmitrovgrad and many other locations are poor, and Russian reassurances have not been persuasive. Similarly, lax safeguards at some facilities inside the former Soviet Union allowed thieves to divert six pounds of 88 percent pure uranium, a safeguards failure widely considered to be the most serious to date. The material, a substantial portion of what a sophisticated bomb builder would need, fortunately was recovered by Czech detectives in December 1994.[59] Finally, lax safeguards at a huge cache of enriched uranium, enough to make twenty or more nuclear bombs, at a fuel fabrication site in Kazakhstan impelled the United States to transport the material to Tennessee.[60] Although the bulk of the material consisted of nuclear waste and alloys not readily usable for bomb making, a significant fraction was uranium 235 fuel for naval nuclear reactors, so highly enriched as to be weapons grade and thus usable in bomb making without further enrichment. (The Kazakh plant mainly fabricates fuel for commercial reactors, which do not use such pure uranium 235.)

The Kazakh episode illustrates that large quantities of weapons-grade as well as weapons-usable material circulate outside the nuclear weapons complex. Although the Kazakh government asserted that the cache was

57. Hibbs, "Plutonium, Politics, and Panic," p. 31. This institute operates a fast breeder reactor and fabricates mixed oxide (MOX) fuel elements.

58. Interview with Gennady Evstafiev by *Yaderny Kontrol*, reprinted in *Monitor* (University of Georgia) (February 1995), p. 10. In the same issue of *Monitor*, p. 6, Victor Mikhailov, the minister of atomic energy, also rebukes German officials for falsely accusing Russia in the incident. He claims that the International Atomic Energy Agency analyzed the material and concluded that it was not of Russian origin.

59. For a recent review of this incident, see Jane Perlez, "Tracing a Nuclear Risk: Stolen Enriched Uranium," *New York Times*, February 15, 1995, p. A3.

60. Michael R. Gordon, "Big Cache of Nuclear Bomb Fuel Found in an Ex-Soviet Republic," *New York Times*, November 23, 1994, p. A1; Stephen Erlanger, "Kazakhstan Thanks U.S. on Uranium," *New York Times*, November 25, 1994, p. A10; and Bill Gertz, "U.S. Defuses Effort by Iran to Get Nukes," *Washington Times*, November 24, 1994, p. 1.

secure in situ and that getting rid of it was an obligation under the Nuclear Non-Proliferation Treaty that Kazakhstan had recently signed, the U.S. government perceived a risk of diversion. That such material could be stolen with relative ease from Minatom or the military is more than hypothetical. A successful theft of naval reactor fuel under military custody actually occurred in late 1993. Three fresh fuel rods containing highly enriched uranium for nuclear submarine reactors disappeared from storage at a Russian military facility in Murmansk. Thieves cut through a padlock, detached a door latch, and removed the fuel rods without detection. The rusty alarm fixtures designed to alert a nearby guard post of intrusion failed.[61] Russian detectives ultimately caught the culprits and recovered the rods.

THREAT OF INSIDE JOBS AND A NUCLEAR MAFIA. By almost all accounts, German officials' pronouncements notwithstanding, the Russian mafia has not been behind any of the incidents of nuclear diversion. The culprits have been small-time opportunists outside the extensive web of organized crime in the former Soviet Union. While bracing for the eventuality, the FBI has not detected any involvement of FSU organized crime groups in any actions or plots to obtain and profit from the sale of nuclear contraband.[62] The Russian Foreign Intelligence Service concurs. Its chief of nonproliferation contends Russia is dealing with nonprofessional petty criminals and that he is "absolutely positive that there is no 'nuclear mafia' analogous to the drug mafia."[63]

The absence of evidence implicating such groups could be a sign of real reluctance to trade in fissionable materials, which indeed are not analogous to illicit drugs. A nuclear underworld would face much greater

---

61. I thank Joshua Handler for information on the Murmansk robbery. A bibliography of references to this incident are in Handler, "Radioactive Waste Situation in the Russian Pacific Fleet, Nuclear Waste Disposal Problems, Submarine Decommissioning, Submarine Safety, and Security of Naval Fuel," Greenpeace Trip Report, Washington, October 27, 1994. Handler describes the security procedures for handling fresh fuel for naval reactors in detail. See especially pp. 27-29.

62. Louis J. Freeh, speech at the Ministry of Internal Affairs Academy, Moscow, July 4, 1994. This ministry, referred to as the MVD, had major custodial responsibilities for nuclear weapons during the early years of the Soviet nuclear program. The MVD and the FSK currently have the major responsibilities for anticorruption investigation and enforcement in Russia.

63. *Monitor* (February 1995), p. 11.

dangers, technical demands, and resistance; criminal organizations have good reasons to avoid this business. Nevertheless, the potential payoffs might present an irresistable temptation to some. Their entry into this market would seem distinctly possible, especially if they can corrupt elements of the FSK that oversee security at nuclear facilities.

Perhaps the gravest risk, as measured by combining the chances of an event with its consequences, is that corrupt FSK and other policing agents would collude with managerial or supervisory personnel at major nuclear facilities in the Minatom complex. Although the odds of such collusion among key personnel might be slim, it cannot be ruled out, and the consequences could certainly be severe. Collusion could result in the clandestine export of sizable stocks of nuclear materials (including plutonium cases from dismantled weapons, for example), the flow of which might go unchecked for a considerable period of time.

No regime of safeguards has ever been devised to deal with an insider game of this scale. U.S. nuclear safeguards for both deployed weapons and nuclear materials are designed to foil only a single insider (a cognizant agent) who may be assisted by outside accomplices.[64] The safeguards degrade ungracefully when they are evaluated against a threat of multiple insiders. Russian safeguards would actually work better than U.S. safeguards in such situations because of the extensive penetration of Russian facilities by FSK personnel charged with ferreting out conspiracies on the inside. But this positive note assumes the integrity of the FSK personnel, and it immediately turns sour if their complicity is assumed instead.

The decisive effect of personnel reliability thus exposes the limitations of security technology and training alone, although technologies to track people and materials at a nuclear facility get some purchase on personnel reliability. The most advanced physical protection hardware and materials control and accounting can be outwitted and circumvented by a team of knowledgeable insiders, particularly by those in custodial positions. The problem of guarding the guardians once again rears its thorny head.

This inherent weakness also exposes the limitations of American assistance in upgrading Russian nuclear safeguards. The United States has provided modern safeguards—access control devices, intrusion sensors,

---

64. This observation on U.S. weapons safeguards is made in Blair, *Logic of Accidental Nuclear War*, p. 283.

even perimeter fences—that have been installed at one high-risk facility (the Kurchatov Institute). A lab-to-lab venture between a U.S. national laboratory and Arzamus-16 has produced a sophisticated safeguards plan applicable throughout the nuclear weapons complex. An agreement has also been reached to cooperate in improving nuclear materials security at six high-risk Minatom facilities.[65] Lastly, the U.S. Nuclear Regulatory Commission and the Russian Nuclear Oversight Committee are working together to develop safety regulations, provide needed equipment for analyzing nuclear materials, and create a national computerized system of accounting for both commercial and military stockpiles of fissionable material.

This technical assistance is judiciously concentrated where it is most needed. At the beneficiary facilities, the number of which will perhaps expand over time, the theft of nuclear materials by an insider will become much harder. Almost all incidents of nuclear theft and smuggling fit this profile. Easy access to materials and easy getaways have emboldened individuals to steal when opportunity knocks. This kind of amateur crime should decline substantially as a result of the redoubled efforts to improve the physical protection of materials and institute new accounting procedures. That the effectiveness of safeguards will ultimately depend on the integrity of the stewardship at the facilities should not detract from the value of these efforts. However, if the stewards yield to the temptation to exploit their positions of trust, no amount of high-technology gadgetry can compensate.

In sum, the risk of nuclear smuggling varies according to the category of material in question and the potential for corruption. My assessment in late 1992 still stands: "Russia especially needs to ensure the security of fissile materials, given that the illicit diversion of even small amounts could result in the spread of nuclear weapons around the world. . . . The military custodians of nuclear weapons pose a smaller security risk than the custodians in charge of safekeeping plutonium and highly enriched uranium (HEU)."[66]

Therefore, Western assistance should concentrate on improving safeguards on Minatom stockpiles of decommissioned weapons and

65. These are Minatom facilities at Electrostal, Novosibirsk, Podolsk, Obninsk, Dimitrovgrad, and Mayak.
66. Blair, *Logic of Accidental Nuclear War*, pp. 259-60.

weapons-grade and weapons-usable fissile materials under its jurisdiction, as well as materials at non-Minatom research facilities. By the same token, the security of nuclear weapons removed from combat delivery systems under a regime of zero alert should be very tight as long as the weapons remain under military custody. The military custodial network in charge of storage depots appears to have retained its basic integrity and cohesion. This gives grounds for confidence in a plan that entails taking thousands of warheads off alert, even if the ultimate fate of weapons turned over for disassembly and storage is less certain. Ironically, international nuclear security might well be better served by a plan that deactivates the nuclear forces and stores the warheads under military guard for an indefinite time.

Russia's Unsafe Strategy of Launch on Warning

Like America's operational strategy for its strategic nuclear forces, Russia's strategy for global nuclear war (whose code word is "sphere") features rapid reaction. Launch on warning has long been the primary retaliation plan for the land-based strategic rocket forces and ballistic missile submarines on pierside alert.[67] The Soviet command and force structure was so geared to this concept that it has been portrayed by Alexei Arbatov as "the one-sided Soviet strategy which relied exclusively on the launch-on-warning principle."[68]

This rapid-reaction strategy falls between the stools of two alternative options: preemption and retaliation after riding out an attack. Preemption has played little or no role in strategic nuclear operations during the past decade and a half.[69] Riding out has been technically

---

67. Blair, *Logic of Accidental Nuclear War*, especially pp. 202-16; and Alexei Arbatov, ed., "Implications of the START II Treaty for US-Russian Relations," report 9, Stimson Center, October 1993, pp. 65-67.

68. Arbatov, "Implications of the START II Treaty," p. 66.

69. The totality of evidence since the late 1970s—heavy Soviet investment in launch on warning and so-called dead hand, or automatic retaliation, arrangements, and heavy emphasis on launch on warning in strategic exercises and training—strongly indicates a preoccupation if not obsession with situations in which the West initiates a strategic nuclear attack. Russian sources, including all former strategic rocket force and submarine officers interviewed by me, considered Soviet strategic nuclear preemption an obsolete option by the late 1970s, and all emphasized the central role of launch on warning in Soviet strategic planning during the 1980s and 1990s.

Many U.S. government analysts contest this interpretation of the evidence. First, while conceding that the Soviets emphasized retaliatory operations in exercises during the 1980s, they argue that retaliation is far more demanding than preemption, that it requires far more training and exercising, and that this visible emphasis does not reflect underlying predilections. But in reality preemption is more difficult than dumb retaliation. It requires extraordinary coordination and smooth execution under conditions of extreme secrecy. One of the U.S. analysts' favorite scenarios of Soviet preemption featured an orchestrated attack by submarines from both northern and Pacific fleets and ICBMs, which would produce a precisely timed sequence of high-altitude electromagnetic pulses over the continental United States starting in the center of the country and working outward. But this extraordinary feat of command and control was far beyond the capability of the Soviet (and Russian) system. If the Soviets did not practice these feats in exercises, which they did not, they simply could not have had confidence in such preemptive options.

U.S. analysts have also identified a class of Russian strategic exercises that they claim features a preemptive option. In these cases a strategic exchange begins with a submarine ballistic missile (SLBM) launch at a time designated in advance. The submarine receives the launch order several hours before launch time. Shortly after the launch, Russian ICBMs fire en masse, followed by additional SLBM and other force strikes, creating the impression of a coordinated preemptive strike led off by a precursor SLBM strike. One recent exercise in this class occurred in spring 1993. A Russian submarine in the Pacific fired an SLBM at a designated time and set off a chain of events that culminated in the real or simulated launch of SLBMs deployed in the northern fleet as part of a strategic exchange with the United States. U.S. government analysts portrayed this exercise as featuring preemption.

But this interpretation is easily refuted. An alternative explanation is that the initial SLBM launch represented the leading edge of a Western first strike; the submarine was playing blue not red in the exercise. This becomes clear because the initial SLBM launch triggers events and timelines that clearly represent a process of Soviet (now Russian) retaliation. The initial launch activates the Russian early warning network, which feeds information to the top-level commanders, who conduct deliberations and authorize a nuclear response, which is disseminated down the chain of command and then carried out by the weapons commanders. Such procedures are undoubtedly associated with retaliation, not preemption. The spring 1993 exercise of the northern fleet submarine force was surely a test of its ability to receive and carry out retaliatory orders in the face of a U.S. first strike paced by a U.S. submarine strike launched from the Pacific Ocean.

Many U.S. government analysts would also contest this assessment of the negligible role of preemption in Russian strategic planning because of sensitivity to the implication that they so exaggerated the importance of Soviet preemption that they distorted the debate over the Strategic Defense Initiative and strategic force modernization. U.S. programs rested squarely on the premise of a coordinated Soviet first strike. Unfortunately, during the professional and public debate over the programs, the intelligence community did not weigh in with its abundant evidence that the Soviet nuclear planning system was almost totally preoccupied with demanding and practically infeasible because of the acute vulnerability of the Russian nuclear command and control system.[70] One credible Russian assessment asserts that "at present, none of the command posts of the highest echelons in Russia could reliably survive a nuclear strike and retain the capability to transmit orders for retaliation."[71] The Soviet military has indeed performed classified computer simulations that have produced the worst possible results: decapitation and total paralysis of the Soviet strategic forces. Statistical artifact or not, the prospect of wartime decapitation deeply concerned Soviet planners.

To compensate for this vulnerability, the Soviets relied on launch on warning, in which a retaliatory decision is made and disseminated before incoming enemy warheads start to explode. This is still the dominant option, though the Russians are striving to shift to launch under attack using the "dead hand," or automatic retaliation system described later. Launch under attack withholds a final retaliatory decision until nuclear explosions from enemy attack are detected. One variant of launch under attack withholds launch authorization until early explosions from incoming submarine-launched ballistic missiles occur; a second variant waits for later ICBM explosions and thus better represents classical second-strike retaliation after riding out an attack.

Both variants of launch under attack have been criticized and resisted by Soviet planners in part because of "the large probability of the complete failure of retaliation because of the preventive decapitation of the command and control system."[72] However, Russian voices advocating a switch to launch under attack are being heard. One such advocate argues that the Russian strategic force structure under START II will shift the bulk of the warheads into the more survivable components—submarines and mobile ICBMs—and "will be less able than today's structure to justify the need for haste in retaliatory actions."[73] While conceding the practical

scenarios in which the West strikes first. The intelligence community in effect repressed a competing view of Soviet strategic motivations and activities, and as a result of this bias the United States pursued what could be considered a dangerously misguided nuclear policy.

70. Blair, *Logic of Accidental Nuclear War*, especially chap. 5.

71. Arbatov, "Implications of the START II Treaty," p. 66.

72. Valery Yarynich, "Nuclear Strategies and the Control Factor," *Segodnya* (March 30, 1994), p. 9, translated in *JPRS-UMA*, April 27, 1994, p. 11.

73. Yarynich, "Nuclear Strategies," p. 11.

impossibility of creating a command system that can ensure retaliation with high confidence, he argues that it appears realistic to create a system providing a 60 to 70 percent confidence level, which he deems adequate for deterrence. The technical feasibility of such a system gives him hope that a strategy of launch under attack can eventually be adopted as the primary basis for deterrence. He believes it "possible that launch on warning and launch under attack could even exchange places in the combat documentation at the command posts of the strategic nuclear forces. That is, launch under attack would become the basic concept and launch on warning an insuring concept."[74]

Although this changeover "cannot be accomplished immediately,"[75] the existing infrastructure of command and control already provides considerable support for the switch to launch under attack for the land-based rocket forces. This infrastructure needs to be substantially upgraded, however, to support other forces, particularly strategic submarines. Until the shift toward a strategy of launch under attack is confidently established, which is unlikely to happen any time soon, if ever, launch on warning will remain the basic concept and predominant option in Russian strategy. The Soviets (and Russians) have deployed and thoroughly exercised all the warning and command and control systems necessary to support this rapid reaction plan.[76]

THE HAIR-TRIGGER TIMELINE OF LAUNCH ON WARNING. After receiving positive attack indications from their infrared satellite or ground radar early warning sensors, the Russian counterpart to the U.S. missile attack warning center at North American Aerospace Defense Command (NORAD) would send a warning report to the headquarters of the defense minister, the general staff, and the strategic rocket force notifying them of an imminent enemy missile strike.[77] The Russian command center for early warning would also

---

74. Yarynich, "Nuclear Strategies," p. 12.

75. Yarynich, "Nuclear Strategies," p. 11.

76. Blair, *Logic of Accidental Nuclear War*, especially chap. 6. The Soviets demonstrated this capability in the early 1980s in exercises that fully integrated satellite-based early warning of a missile attack with the nuclear command system.

77. The early warning satellites are focused on U.S. and Chinese ICBM fields and could detect a missile launch about one minute after liftoff. The data would be downlinked at site E21 near the Moscow beltway (E-ring) and automatically forwarded via cable links to the Russian NORAD equivalent (the Center for Analysis of Missile and Space Situation) at Venyukovski inside the beltway. Over-

transmit a special warning signal to the president, defense minister, and chief of the general staff through their nuclear suitcase, whose handlers (general staff personnel from the Ninth Directorate, called shuriks) would immediately notify them of the emergency. Within four to six minutes after liftoff, the top leadership including the Russian president, defense minister, chief of the general staff, and the nuclear commanders in chief, along with the chief of the early warning center, should convene an emergency teleconference over special communications reserved for this circumstance.[78] (These procedures appear to have been implemented during a recent incident in which the launch of a Norwegian scientific rocket apparently triggered a false alarm of a missile attack.)[79] Then if the early warning network provides dual sensor confirmation of an enemy missile

the-horizon ground radar can detect and report to the Venyukovski center a mass ICBM liftoff almost as rapidly. Ground radar stations on the periphery of the former Soviet Union would also report detection of SLBM launches to the center. The Venyukovski center would form a missile attack warning message and send it over cable links to the general staff main war room in Moscow, the SRF main war room near the village of Perkhushkovo and town of Odintsovo, and the defense minister at his Moscow headquarters (inside the general staff headquarters), as well as to designated alternative wartime command posts. Displays at those locations would indicate the size and character of the attack. The center would also signal the nuclear suitcases of the president, defense minister, and chief of the general staff if they were away from their wartime posts, alerting them of an imminent strike.

78. At this time the political leadership of Ukraine, Belarus, and Kazakhstan are also supposed to be tied into the emergency decisionmaking conference over a special telephone communications system (KAVKAZ, which is part of the KAZBEK network) installed for this purpose. This requirement doubtless would be among the first casualties of any serious emergency.

79. The missile flew from northern Norway to Spitzbergen on January 25, 1995. Norway had given advance notification of the upcoming rocket launch to the Russian Ministry of Defense, and its trajectory took it no closer than 150 miles from Russian territory during its northerly flight. Nevertheless, the initial detection presumably by missile warning radar on Russia's northern periphery apparently caused some confusion about the missile's destination.

President Yeltsin described the incident as follows: "Yesterday I used my 'attache case' for the first time [he was clearly referring to the black box]. I called the defense minister and the relevant services and asked them what kind of missile it was and where it had come from. Within a minute I had the information—the entire flight of the missile had been monitored from start to finish. We had calculated that it would fall somewhere far from our shores. We therefore did not shoot it down— they [probably referring to the Norwegians] clearly did not expect us to detect the

attack, the general staff together with certain senior nuclear commanders, especially the commander in chief of the SRF, would transmit a preliminary command that activates the previously disconnected communications links used to disseminate any subsequent launch orders.[80] The attack confirmation from the early warning center is supposed to be a technical precondition for issuing this preliminary command, in which case the establishment of the channel used to send the unlock and launch authorization codes could be partially outside the control of the general staff and strategic force commanders.

The Russian national command authority (president and defense minister) would then deliberate under a strict time limit—no more than three minutes. Using their voice teleconference network along with their famous nuclear suitcases (if they are not already ensconced in the wartime command bunkers), the national decisionmakers would give (or withhold) approval (a permission command) to launch a retaliatory strike to the general staff and three senior nuclear commanders (commanders of the SRF, navy, and air force) in the field.[81] If communications with both the president and defense

missile on our radar. Maybe somebody had decided to test us out?" *Izvestiya*, January 27, 1995, p. 1, in Foreign Broadcast Information Service, *Daily Report: Soviet Union*, January 27, 1995, p. 18; Doug Clarke, "Yeltsin Makes Best of Missile False Alarm," *OMRI Daily Digest*, No. 20, pt. 1, January 27, 1995; and Clarke, "Defense Ministry Said to Have Been Told about Norwegian Missile," *OMRI Daily Digest*, No. 22, pt. 1, January 31, 1995.

80. The preliminary command also initiates a host of precautionary alert steps: bombers take off, submarines hide in deep water, mobile ICBMs in transit scurry to the nearest presurveyed or other launch sites, and units adopt cover and concealment practices. The actual steps taken would depend on the readiness of the forces, which in turn would depend on prior alert declarations. Four alert levels for Soviet (and Russian) strategic forces exist: constant, increased, military threat, and full. The normal peacetime level is constant. This system puts ICBMs in silos only a few minutes from full alert status, at which point their launch reaction time would be 1.5 minutes. For mobile ICBMs, constant alert means that about 20 percent are deployed in the field (one regiment out of a given division) and the remainder are in garrison. At increased alert (the level usually declared during past crises), the bombers would be loaded with nuclear weapons and the mobile ICBMs in garrison would be primed for launch on warning. If a military threat were declared, the mobile ICBMs would leave their shelters and travel to preset hide or launch sites. At full alert, the mobile ICBMs achieve a launch reaction time of 2.5 minutes.

81. The nuclear suitcase is called CHEGET, which is part of the KAZBEK network. The nuclear suitcases might be designed to transmit to the general staff

minister are severed, the chief of the general staff acting alone could authorize retaliation by various means, including the dead hand system.

Permission to retaliate would normally have to be obtained from the national command authorities within about ten minutes after enemy missile liftoff to launch on warning successfully. Then the general staff would form and disseminate the launch order replete with unlock codes; this procedure takes two or three minutes.[82] By this time twelve to thirteen minutes would have elapsed since enemy missile liftoff.

main war room a part of the overall code that would unblock the strategic nuclear forces. If the president is on-line, his permission might be sufficient to authorize retaliation. (A Russian preemptive attack likely requires permission from both the president and the defense minister.) If communications with the president and his immediate successor (the prime minister) are severed, permission from the defense minister alone might suffice. In the event of a complete failure of communications with the national command authorities, the chief of the general staff likely could exercise launch authority under conditions of verified attack (presence of nuclear detonations) directly or through the dead hand system.

The notion that the president's and defense minister's nuclear suitcases perform a critical enabling as well as authorizing function and therefore represent a formidable safeguard against unauthorized launches by the general staff is weakened by several factors. First, the communications outages that allow control to devolve to the general staff can be simulated by pulling the plug on the links, as happened during the 1991 coup. (Links to Gorbachev's nuclear suitcase were severed by the coup plotters; the Ninth Directorate sector handlers packed up the suitcase and returned it to the general staff headquarters.) Second, provisions are surely made for the general staff to effect an immediate launch if the suitcases malfunction or the national command authorities forget their codes or otherwise fumble the equipment. An electromechanical malfunction would surely not prevent the general staff from quickly sending out the enabling and authorizing codes upon hearing the president authorize a launch during the emergency voice telecommunications conference with his top military commanders. By the same token, his withholding of launch authorization would not technically preclude launch. Third, the general staff's ninth sector is responsible for inputting the codes into the nuclear suitcases when they are initially assigned to the national command authorities. This implies that the general staff has access to them at all stages of the operation. However, organizational safeguards within the general staff, perhaps involving personnel (for example, from the FSK) outside military control, might serve to keep the Ninth Directorate separated from the main operations directorate responsible for launching the strategic forces.

82. The formation and dissemination of this launch order normally requires the active participation of the commander of the nuclear forces. To launch ICBMs, for example, the general staff would send the launch code to the commander in chief of

The general staff can elect to disseminate launch commands by either of two methods.[83] One is to pass the unblock and launch codes directly to the individual launch crews who carry out the order. For the ICBMs the general staff can deliver the launch order to the regimental launch posts in fifteen seconds. The crews require three minutes to receive, verify, and confirm the dispatch and another few minutes to implement it. Russian ICBMs would thus fire out of their silos in less than twenty minutes from the time of the initial enemy missile launch.[84]

The second method is to bypass the subordinate command posts and deliver the launch order directly to the launch platforms, for example, the launch equipment in the unmanned silos (SS-18s) or on the mobile transport erectors (SS-25s). From its war room, the general staff could turn the launch keys that signal the unmanned rockets to fire from their silos or truck launchers. The rocket equipment can process the unlock and

the strategic rocket forces, who would process it electronically and then transmit it back to a node of the general staff, where the two inputs would be combined, encrypted, and disseminated over the basic automated command system (BACSAN), another integral element of the KAZBEK network. If the SRF headquarters were destroyed beforehand, the general staff working alone could send the codes that trigger launch. BACSAN is tied into large computer centers that modify attack plans and if necessary compute new flight trajectories for missiles.

BACSAN employs primary and reserve communications using cable, radio, satellites, troposcatter, and other links, and it automatically switches from damaged to reserve channels in seconds. All channels are encrypted. In addition, BACSAN is integrated with a backup system known as the duplicating radio command system (DRCS). This system consists of one-way radio channels linking the nuclear commanders to the ICBM regiments, the bombers, and submarines. It primarily uses satellites, high-frequency radio, and very low to extremely low frequency radio stations. A common center manages the many transmitters to choose the optimal frequency for the conditions in various regions and to ensure that the different frequencies work synchronously.

83. Both methods use BACSAN, which employs terminals placed on all strategic command posts as well as all bombers, submarines, and ICBMs in silos or on mobile transport erector launchers.

84. These estimates come from Russian experts. The West has monitored Soviet strategic exercises in which ICBMs lifted off twenty-one minutes after the simulated onset of Western missile attack. In the event of an enemy strike that hits the Russian missile fields and disrupts local launch procedures before missiles can be fired, provisions have been made to switch to backup launch centers and communications channels.

launch signals and ignite the booster within about five minutes after receiving the command. Using this method, which became operational in 1976, the general staff can thus trigger a mass retaliatory salvo in less than twenty minutes from the onset of an enemy missile strike.

Both launch methods support launch on warning. Both timelines beat the arrival of incoming U.S. ICBMs by ten minutes. Yet the Russians lack confidence in these methods.[85] The West could, for instance, beat the timeline using forward-deployed submarine missiles with flight times as short as fifteen minutes. The Russian early warning system has gaping holes in its coverage of submarine launch areas.[86] Precursor strikes by nuclear bombers or submarines against critical nodes in the Russian command system could escape unnoticed until it was too late. Attack indications from the early warning network, which has been put in jeopardy of being splintered by the breakup of the Soviet Union, could be absent, ambiguous, or false. Political leaders could hesitate too long before authorizing retaliation. The list goes on.

DEAD HAND AND LAUNCH UNDER ATTACK. The problems of launch on warning inspired the development of another method of strategic launch. Conforming to the principle of launch under attack, it has been dubbed the dead hand by Russians familiar with it. Developed during the 1970s and fully operational by 1985, this last-ditch method of launch dissemination has been described in considerable detail elsewhere.[87] Suffice it here to outline the main features.

85. See Blair, *Logic of Accidental Nuclear War,* for a longer discussion of this issue.

86. This is a critical shortcoming. See the discussion of the Trident D-5 SLBM threat in a later section. The incident involving the Norwegian scientific rocket discussed earlier appears to crystallize the problem of SLBM attack warning. The launch area of the Norwegian Sea is poorly monitored by Russian early warning satellites, and the flight time of nuclear-armed missiles fired from there at Moscow would be less than twenty minutes. The Norwegian rocket's apogee was about 900 miles, which closely corresponds to the maximum altitude of a Trident D-5 SLBM fired at Moscow from the Norwegian Sea. Russian radar apparently initially miscalculated the Norwegian rocket's flight path, resulting in the immediate alerting of the Russian nuclear decisionmakers because of Russia's vulnerability to sudden strikes through this corridor.

87. Bruce G. Blair, "Russia's Doomsday Machine," *New York Times,* October 8, 1993, p. A35; and William J. Broad, "Russia Has Computerized Nuclear 'Doomsday' Machine, U.S. Expert Says," *New York Times,* October 8, 1993, p. A6.

After detecting nuclear missiles headed in the direction of Moscow or in anticipation of a possible decapitation strike, the Russian leadership could choose to activate a reserve command system designed to ensure massive Russian retaliation if the expected attack actually materializes. This dead hand reserve system would be activated by a "fail deadly" message sent by the general staff from its main war room to a more survivable underground command node outside Moscow. (Duplicate nodes were built between 1985 and the early 1990s.) This message would contain a component of the unlocking codes necessary to launch the strategic forces. If after receiving this message the node subsequently experienced a complete break in communications with the general staff and if sensors ringing the node detected nuclear explosions, the team assembled there would be automatically enabled to form and distribute a complete launch message to the dispersed strategic forces.[88]

This team consists of a skeleton staff in residence under normal peacetime conditions. If time and circumstances permit, senior officials of government (at the level of deputy defense minister, for example) could relocate there under emergency conditions. Whatever its composition, however, the team lacks the discretionary authority to make the retaliatory decision; that is the point of the three requirements noted above. At the same time, the team must perform certain tasks for the dead hand system to work as designed. If it fails to carry out these duties, the system remains dormant.

Once the technical prerequisites are satisfied, this special node would use a collocated underground low-frequency antenna to radio a launch order with unblock codes. The order would be received by command rockets in silos (special SS-17s) or on trucks (special SS-25s, formerly SS-20s) within range of the low-frequency radio signal, about 600 miles. The special command rockets would then automatically launch (after a short delay) on different trajectories and relay the order from space to the dispersed nuclear-armed bombers, ICBMs, and submarines (the latter via naval shore transmitters such as the Kola extra-low-frequency station serving the Northern fleet submarine force).[89]

88. The communications outage must persist for a certain period of time and the sensors detect nuclear detonations using visual, seismic, radiation, and overpressure instruments.

89. The SS-25 and SS-17 command rockets transmit for 20 to 50 minutes over ultrahigh-frequency channels to all the regions of strategic force deployment in the former Soviet Union. The range constraint of UHF is limited only by line of sight.

For mobile or silo-based nuclear ICBMs, the signals from the command rockets would trigger an automatic launch unless the individual missiles are still connected to their parent regimental launch control centers. If the local links remain intact, the command rocket signals would be received by the regimental posts, which would then perform the launch procedures. If the links have been severed by enemy strikes, the missiles in the unmanned silos would receive the launch order directly from the command rockets and automatically fire after a short delay. If the nuclear-tipped mobile SS-25 missiles with local firing crews have lost contact with higher authority, the missiles would receive the launch order directly and automatically fire from their transport erector launchers at presurveyed sites.[90]

The rationale for this dead hand system is evident. It backs up the two main variants of launch on warning in which the national command authorities and general staff would attempt to authorize retaliation and disseminate the order before incoming enemy missiles wrecked havoc on the command system. A backup arrangement was deemed necessary because the main methods might not work under a wide range of plausible adverse conditions. The idea was to transfer the executive function to more survivable elements of the command system in anticipation of a decapitation strike so that fairly prompt retaliation could be ensured even if the top leadership perished before it could personally order retaliation using the two main methods. Under this plan, retaliation would take a few tens of minutes longer than launch on warning.

The principle of the dead hand thus implies that the general staff would activate it at the critical moment in the launch-on-warning cycle, which would occur between six and ten minutes after enemy missile liftoff. If by ten minutes after liftoff the top leaders still do not have a clear enough picture of the attack, or if the civilian leadership would fail for any reason to give timely authorization to retaliate, the general staff could resort to the dead hand system to ensure quasi-automatic retaliation in the event of their own annihilation.

Approval to activate it could be obtained from the national command authority before any final decision on retaliation is rendered and before any damage sustained from enemy submarine-based missiles. Approval

---

90. After receiving the command rocket signal, the launchers automatically level themselves and raise and fire the missile.

might be given earlier in a nuclear crisis if Russia would suffer a degradation of its early warning or command system performance due to conventional hostilities or other strains. In any case, presidential or defense minister approval would not be technically essential; the general staff evidently could activate the dead hand on its own accord, as it might have to do if it loses contact with both the president and defense minister.

LAUNCH ON WARNING AND DEAD HAND: SAFETY ISSUES. The Russian strategic posture is clearly geared to rapid retaliation in response to attack indications from early warning networks and nuclear explosion sensors. It is impossible to gauge precisely the adverse effects on nuclear weapons safety, but the crisis preparations undertaken to ensure prompt retaliation surely increase the risk of inadvertent or unauthorized launch.

In broad outline the two methods of nuclear release associated with launch on warning appear to run a greater risk than the backup dead hand method because launch on warning impels decisionmakers to make the fateful decision in a few minutes on the basis of sensor reports of imminent attack. Given the many imperfections of warning systems and other strains on the decision process, launch on warning is not an option that meets high standards of nuclear weapons safety. As a Russian expert and former officer in the strategic rocket forces has noted, "the very idea of an immediate and impulsive nuclear reaction to the information from technical means of warning (even if they are 'absolutely' reliable) seems absurd."[91]

From the standpoint of safety it would be more prudent for the Russians to withhold a launch decision, activate the dead hand in response to tactical warning, and predicate a final launch order on evidence of nuclear explosions. To the extent that Russian decisionmakers feel confident in its working, the dead hand alleviates some of the pressure to launch on warning. It also at least imposes a set of objective conditions, especially evidence of nuclear detonations, that supposedly must be satisfied before launch authorization is disseminated. In sum, launch under attack using the dead hand permits an initial mistake (false alarm or misinterpretation of warning sensor data) to be corrected by the absence of nuclear explosions; launch on warning is less tolerant of initial error because an irrevocable launch decision might be based on the same

91. Yarynich, "Nuclear Strategies," p. 11.

mistake that only activates the dead hand system.[92] The design and functioning of this system remain too obscure, however, to offer any more than this superficial evaluation of its safety. (Indeed, some skeptics doubt its very existence.[93])

92. In an apparent reference to the dead hand, Valery Yarynich makes this point in saying that launch under attack gives decisionmakers the right to make a mistake, whereas launch on warning does not. See "Nuclear Strategies," p. 11. In another article, Yarynich elaborates the same point: "The point of this 'doomsday system' is that Russia's top commanders will not be forced to launch nuclear missiles immediately after receiving a signal that Moscow is under attack. On receiving such a signal—which could turn out to be false—the general staff can quickly transfer its capability to launch nuclear missiles to the equipment and crew in the radio station. . . . If there is no attack, the doomsday system will return to its initial state. From a purely technical point of view, this system is more likely to reduce the probability of a tragic mistake than to increase it." "The Doomsday Machine's Safety Catch," *New York Times*, February 1, 1994, p. A17.

93. In addition to my original sources and Yarynich's "Doomsday Machine's Safety Catch," at least four knowledgeable Russian sources have recently provided pertinent information that bolsters my contention that the Soviets developed and deployed a dead hand system to ensure nuclear retaliation. All of the sources independently confirmed that the Soviet Union developed the system, which included a quasi-automatic trigger governed by nuclear explosion sensors and a number of other components such as command rockets. All of them referred to this system as a dead hand. They were divided, however, over the question whether the quasi-automatic trigger feature of the system was actually put on-line.

Two sources asserted categorically that the end-to-end system was operationally deployed. One of these two was a central figure in the overall system's development. The other was a senior civilian working-level official in the military-industrial complex who possessed a refined comprehension of the system. He distinguished between two variants of the command rocket system: the dead hand variant involving the unblocking by sensor trigger and the other variant involving the direct loading and firing of the command rockets by the general staff from their command posts. He asserted that both variants were provided for by the operational system.

Two other sources claimed that the command rockets were deployed in variant two (configured to enable the general staff to load launch instructions into them and fire them by remote control), but that the option of falling back on a sensor-driven quasi-automatic trigger was not made operational despite strong support from its proponents. One of these two was connected with the main operations directorate of the general staff during the 1980s. The other was highly placed in the Ministry of General Machine Building. This civilian claimed that Marshall Sergei Akhromeyev, chief of the general staff under Gorbachev, overrode a recommendation by the Central Committee of the Communist party for deploying the quasi-automatic sensor trigger on the grounds that it was too dangerous, and that Akhromeyev

But in the final analysis all the command and control arrangements discussed here sustain alert practices and emergency launch procedures whose main purpose is to service deterrence, not safety. If the priorities were reversed and safety became paramount, these arrangements would not survive evaluation. The operational posture would have to eliminate its dependence on strategic and tactical warning, and on strategies of launch on warning and launch under attack. Delayed retaliation measured in many hours or days would replace prompt retaliation. Strategic forces would be taken off alert and the hair trigger removed from the nuclear command system.

A symbolic step in this direction was taken when the nuclear superpowers agreed in early 1994 to aim their missiles away from their cold war targets and instead point them at the oceans. This agreement applies only to those strategic missiles that must have target data in their computer memory to maintain launch readiness: Minuteman III and older classes of Russian ICBMs. The MX missiles and U.S. SLBMs, as well as some of the newest classes of Russian ICBMs, do not normally hold target data even when they maintain a high level of launch readiness, and hence this scheme did not affect them. In any case, the United States and doubtless Russia, too, has the ability to restore the wartime targets in seconds.[94] And both continue to rely on postures of rapid reaction that pose very demanding problems of safety for the nuclear command and control systems.

Zero alert offers a genuine solution to the dangers posed by hair-trigger postures that require excessive speed and flawless performance in nuclear warning, decisionmaking, and launch equipment and procedures.

rejected it on the advice of the central figure in the system's development cited earlier (the same person who claimed the entire system was actually deployed).

It seems that the U.S. intelligence community's position is that the dead hand was developed but never deployed operationally (except for the command rockets). Considering the community's original skepticism, which basically dismissed the whole story, and lack of knowledge about the command rocket system (it did not know that these rockets could directly fire the fixed and mobile ICBMs without any assistance from launch crews in the missile fields), the intelligence community bears the burden of proof that the dead hand never became operational.

94. Basically, the launch crews enter a single number into the launch control computer before launch, instructing missiles to change their trajectories in flight so that their warheads land on wartime targets instead of nominal ocean targets. Further technical details are provided later.

The Risk of Nuclear Anarchy

The overall risk of nuclear anarchy is made up of the components examined here, the ranking of which should take into account both their probabilities and consequences. An integrative judgment that combines these elements is intrinsically difficult, but certain tentative conclusions emerge from the exercise.

The events of lowest probability are the unauthorized use of nuclear weapons by rogue field commanders and the seizure of operational control of nuclear weapons by Ukraine. By comparison, the highest probabilities are nuclear smuggling, particularly the diversion of material from the civilian sector under Minatom control and the sudden breakdown of nuclear control at the top levels of command in Moscow. The inadvertent launch of nuclear missiles on hair-trigger alert during a crisis has an intermediate probability that varies according to the state of nuclear tensions between Russia and its potential nuclear adversaries, particularly the United States.

Combining the potential consequences of these events with their probabilities leaves little doubt that political upheaval in Moscow, which could buckle the entire nuclear chain of command, poses the gravest overall danger. As I argued in an earlier analysis, the multitude of nuclear control problems in the FSU is

> overshadowed by a weakness inherent in any nuclear command system but one of particular concern in the Russian system at this juncture: the potential unreliability of the apex of nuclear command. No command and control system can stand apart from the foibles and mischief of persons who hold, or seize, the top positions of leadership. The system reflects their virtues or lack thereof; and its effectiveness depends on their legitimacy, loyalty, and competence. These are the guardians of the nuclear arsenal. The malevolence, corruption, or greed of a few of them could sweep aside a regime of safeguards.[95]

An antiballistic missile system offers scant relief. It might protect U.S. territory from very small scale unauthorized attacks by individual renegade weapons commanders, but that kind of event is among the least

---

95. Blair, *Logic of Accidental Nuclear War*, p. 260.

likely. More plausible possibilities involve medium- or large-scale attacks that would overwhelm antiballistic missile deployments. Invoking the threat of nuclear anarchy to justify a strategic ABM program therefore puts a heavy burden of proof on the sponsor. (The destabilizing effects increase the burden.)

Zero alert offers a superior alternative to ABM. Taking all nuclear weapons off alert so that none remain poised for immediate launch is the ounce of prevention for nuclear anarchy in all its many forms. A reciprocal agreement among the nuclear weapon states to adopt zero alert for all nuclear forces would be the most effective hedge against the collapse of Russian command and control.

Tensing the Nuclear Postures: The Pentagon's Plan

Despite witnessing the incipient stages of nuclear anarchy in the former Soviet Union, the U.S. defense establishment remains fervently oriented to its traditional cold war mission of deterring the leadership of the Russian government from launching a deliberate attack. The attention the Pentagon gives to addressing the safety of nuclear weapons operations, particularly Russian operations, pales by comparison to its commitment to classical deterrence.

As the Russian nuclear command and control system strains to preserve cohesion, the central theme of U.S. nuclear planning is to hedge against a takeover of power by reactionary leaders who would set off a new cycle of nuclear confrontation with the West. The Pentagon's specific blueprint, the nuclear posture review (NPR), for hedging the nuclear future unfortunately will only increase the strain on the Russian command and control system and thereby degrade safety.

The NPR, a yearlong study completed in fall 1994, did make significant observations and recommendations relevant to improving the safety of U.S. and Russian nuclear operations.[96] Regarding U.S. forces, it noted that the army no longer possesses nuclear weapons, the navy no longer deploys nonstrategic nuclear weapons at sea, all strategic bombers have been taken off alert, and fewer submarines patrol on full alert at sea.

---

96. Unless indicated otherwise, information about the NPR and its findings draw on an official briefing document: Department of Defense, "Nuclear Posture Review," September 22, 1994.

In addition, ICBMs and SLBMs have been detargeted (a misnomer discussed later), the active stockpiles of strategic and nonstrategic warheads have shrunk (59 percent since 1988 and will shrink a total of 71 percent by 2003, the number of nuclear storage locations has dropped by 75 percent, and the number of personnel with access to or control of nuclear weapons has declined by 70 percent. The review recommends correcting deficiencies in missile attack early warning systems, equipping the U.S. Trident submarine force with a safeguard that requires the crew to receive instructions from external sources in order to be physically able to fire its missiles, and upgrading the comparable safeguards already in use on the B-52 bomber and Minuteman III missile forces.

With respect to Russian nuclear safety, the NPR considered initiatives ranging from removing warheads from all Russian ICBMs to cooperating with the United States in verifying the alert status of nuclear forces. The main safety recommendation was to continue to support the program of cooperative threat reduction (popularly known as the Nunn-Lugar program) to assist the FSU in dismantling nuclear weapons and preventing the illicit diversion of weapons or fissionable materials. Under this rubric the Pentagon has established closer ties with the Russian military to help build mutual trust with military leaders whose tenure could easily outlast that of current civilian political leaders.

The recommendations for improving U.S. nuclear safety are worthy but wholly inadequate. Correcting deficiencies in tactical early warning, however desirable, slides past the crux of the safety problem: excessive speed in nuclear decisionmaking and launch procedures. Basing nuclear strategy on rapid reaction or literal launch on warning is inherently risky, and only in part because early warning networks cannot be made infallible.

The prescribed installation of new physical safeguards on Trident submarines, and the upgrading of similar safeguards on the B-52 bombers and Minuteman III missiles are also desirable but not decisive measures. The specific idea for Trident is to lock up a vital enabling component such as a key for the missile launching system in a safe on board the submarines. To retrieve the key, the crew would need a code from higher authority that would open the safe. This code, however, would probably be little more than the combination for one of two locks on the safe, so the safeguard might not be that difficult to circumvent. Second, the upgraded safeguards for bombers and land-based missiles will surely still involve a limited set of codes that, although held by higher authorities, are subject to compromise.[97] These codes, as well as those for the Trident submarines, will continue to be widely dispersed within the nuclear chain of command in peacetime and will be the same digits as those that would be dialed into the locking devices by low-level weapons commanders. In other words, the upgrade of safeguards on the weapons will not solve the problem of safeguarding the codes themselves, a point driven home by a December 1994 incident in which the extant unlock codes for strategic forces were compromised aboard a U.S. Strategic Command airborne command center. Third, these safety recommendations are to be grafted onto weapons set on a hair trigger, which is like improving a safety catch on a loaded, cocked, and aimed weapon.

But the greatest irony is that the improvements for U.S. forces recommended by the NPR and endorsed by President Clinton will likely erode instead of promote the safety of Russian nuclear operations. As they have done for the past several years, U.S. deployments will probably induce the Russian command system to further shorten the fuse on Russian strategic forces. Dangerous operational shortcuts will continue to be taken to compensate for what Russian planners perceive as a growing American potential for a disarming first strike.

Russia's Unstable Nuclear Posture

Russian strategists, who, like their American counterparts, remain committed to deterrence despite the breakthrough in political relations between the countries, worry about a multitude of threats that increase the vulnerability of their strategic forces. These include attacks on mobile SS-24 and SS-25 land-based missiles by precision-guided conventional munitions delivered by Western aircraft, antisubmarine warfare conducted against Russian submarines in the Barents and Okhotsk Seas, sabotage of mobile land-based missiles by Western special operations forces, and strikes by conventional munitions against the large unprotected radio station on the Kola Peninsula used to communicate with deeply submerged submarines. The main source of Russian anxiety,

---

97. One of the major deficiencies of the current unlock codes for these forces is that a single short code can unlock all the missiles. The recommended upgrade presumably will provide for unlocking subsets of the forces on a selective basis.

however, is the ongoing U.S. deployment of Trident submarines armed with highly accurate D-5 missiles. The first two of these became operational as the Berlin Wall was falling in 1989. Currently there are seven submarines carrying a total of 168 D-5 missiles and 1,344 warheads.

THE BANE OF RUSSIAN PLANNING. The Trident D-5 force alone, representing only 18 percent of the active U.S. strategic nuclear stockpile (1,344 out of 7,700 warheads), poses a qualitatively new threat to Russia. The missile's pinpoint accuracy means that practically any target in Russia except a handful of underground command bunkers is vulnerable to destruction by U.S. SLBMs, even though most D-5s carry warheads with relatively low explosive power.[98] These vulnerable targets include all the primary command centers (as opposed to backup posts deep underground) of the political leadership, general staff, and nuclear commanders in chief; all operational ICBM silos (approximately 570), mobile ICBM forces in garrison and associated ICBM launch control centers at the regimental and division levels; all submarines in port; and all strategic bombers at their primary bases.[99]

Accuracy aside, this U.S. force poses a new threat because of its short time of flight. Targets have thus become vulnerable to sudden destruction. Departing their home port in Kings Bay, Georgia, the submarines could move to launch stations in the Norwegian Sea, from which a Trident D-5 missile fired at Moscow would land in fifteen minutes.[100] If directly

98. Of the current D-5 warhead inventory, 944 warheads are W76 types that produce a yield of 100 kilotons, and 400 are W88 types that yield 475 kilotons. All warheads to be deployed on the D-5 missile in the future will be W76 types.

99. This assessment assumes five Trident D-5 submarines at sea carrying a total of 960 warheads, of which 768 are deliverable given an overall launch and flight reliability of 80 percent. Each delivered warhead has a 100 percent probability of destroying its target (a debatable but quite defensible assumption). Submarines are presumably positioned at launch locations within range of all strategic targets on Russian territory (with a D-5 missile range of 7,000 miles, forward-deployed boats near Europe in the North Atlantic Ocean and Norwegian Sea could cover the entire Russian and FSU land mass).

100. For a D-5 missile armed with eight high-yield W88 warheads, the flight time for striking targets at a range of 2,000 miles would be nineteen minutes. For closer targets located, say, 1,000 miles away, the flight time would be just under thirteen minutes. At the 4,000 mile maximum range for this missile package (D-5s with eight W88s), the flight time would be twenty-eight minutes.

targeted, critical facilities in the nuclear command system in the Moscow area would stand little chance of surviving.

For Russian planners, the significance of these short flight times is that the United States might be able to deprive them of their principal retaliatory option, launch on warning, which takes a minimum of twelve minutes to authorize and disseminate under ideal conditions and additional time for strategic weapons commanders to implement. A total of nearly twenty minutes is needed to exercise the option. Although this response is rapid (so rapid as to be unsafe), it still might not be fast enough for Russian missiles to escape destruction on the ground.

A response time of twenty minutes left a little time to spare in the days when only U.S. ICBMs with their twenty-five to thirty minute flight times were accurate enough to destroy protected Russian command posts and hard missile silos. In those days, U.S. submarine missiles could have struck more quickly but not as accurately. Today the Russian command system, even while operating in a quasi-automatic decision mode, might not have enough time to get out the message before being suppressed, or at best it would just barely beat the deadline. Even so, the D-5 missiles could still reach and destroy many of the strategic forces at fixed locations in Ukraine and European Russia, including many silo-based ICBMs as well as mobile ICBMs in garrison and submarines on alert in port, before they could carry out the launch orders.

Targets located farther east and south would stand a better chance of survival. D-5 missiles stationed near Europe and aimed at ICBMs in Kazakhstan, Russian Siberia, and the Far East would arrive twenty to thirty minutes after launch, which might be early enough, or slightly too late, to catch the missiles on the ground.[101] Under ideal response conditions, much of the Russian ICBM force in these regions, notably the six SS-18 fields that house the core force of Russian ICBMs, should be able to beat the clock, but at most only by a few minutes.

Even this slim margin may be erased when Trident D-5 missiles become operational in the Pacific. Current plans call for increasing D-5 deployments from 168 missiles (944 warheads) on 7 submarines to 336

---

101. In addition to longer flight times, the D-5 launches would be staggered, with time intervals of twenty seconds between each. The last of the Trident's twenty-four missiles would thus fire eight minutes after the first was launched, giving the Russian force additional time to respond.

missiles (1,680 warheads) on 14 submarines by 2003. Seven of the submarines will likely be stationed at Bangor, Washington (leaving seven at Kings Bay), from which they can move into position to cover strategic targets in the eastern half of the FSU and China.[102] With submarines in the Atlantic covering targets in the western half, all targets in the FSU could be struck in twenty minutes or less. Russia simply could not exercise launch on warning this quickly unless operational shortcuts that further compromise safety were instituted.

The strain on Russian nuclear decisionmaking caused by Trident D-5 deployments is great enough without considering another complication: deficient Russian early warning of missile attack. Potential D-5 launch points in the North Atlantic and Pacific Oceans and the Norwegian Sea, and their associated flight corridors into Russia, lie outside the coverage of Russia's workhorse early warning satellites.[103] The elliptical orbits of the satellites enable them to focus only on U.S. ICBM and Chinese land-based missile fields, while newer geostationary satellites designed to detect SLBM launches from waters close to Russia might be plagued by infrared sensor flaws and in any case do not appear to be operational. Satellites in geostationary orbits probably will not become mainstays in the Russian early warning network for many years to come. Ground-based warning radar thus carries the burden of detecting a Trident D-5 missile attack.

Radar coverage of potential corridors of Trident attack depends heavily on older Hen House radars on the Russian northern periphery and on Latvian and Ukrainian territory. Plans to construct modern radars in Latvia and Ukraine to provide reliable early detection of Trident SLBM strikes have been canceled or postponed. A modern radar to be located in Siberia to cover Trident launches from the Pacific was also canceled. In consequence, Russian early warning of Trident D-5 attack depends on an antiquated and politically fragmented network of ground-based radars

102. Eric Rosenberg, "Navy Readies New Trident Submarine Basing Strategy," *Defense Week*, February 21, 1995, p. 5.

103. An excellent technical overview of the Russian satellite early warning network is provided in Paul Podvig, "The Operational Status of the Russian Space-Based Early Warning System," *Science and Global Security*, vol. 4 (1994), pp. 363-84. This article also provides useful information about Russian ground-radar warning systems.

whose warning reports cannot be reliably confirmed by a space-based tier of sensors. Early warning is so unreliable for such an attack that launch on warning becomes both more dangerous from the standpoint of safety and less feasible from the standpoint of deterrence.

Russian planners worry even more about the Trident D-5 threat because of the deteriorating combat readiness of their theoretically least vulnerable strategic forces, submarines and mobile SS-24 and SS-25 land-based missiles. Shortages of manpower, spare parts, and maintenance have curtailed sea patrols and mobile land missile operations out of garrison. Almost all submarines have been confined to port, where some are routinely geared for launch on warning to mitigate their acute vulnerability.[104] The trainborne SS-24 missiles have also been sidelined; some are likely primed for quick launch for the same reason. The vast majority of the truck-based SS-25 missiles have been confined to garrison, where they too can be kept ready for quick launch. The small number of SS-25s operating covertly in field locations exploit mobility for protection from sudden attack, but they too are afflicted with readiness problems, limiting the numbers on day-to-day field alert and hampering the ability of SS-25 forces in garrison to disperse rapidly in a crisis.

In sum, most of the Russian mobile strategic forces that would be survivable under normal circumstances have been grounded. They have become vulnerable targets that depend more heavily on launch on warning for their survival than do the immobile ICBMs in silos. This operational shortcut further erodes classical strategic stability as well as safety. And the diminishing feasibility of launch on warning in the face of Trident D-5 deployments magnifies Russia's distress over its strategic vulnerability.

RUSSIAN FEARS OF DISARMING STRIKES. If the launch-on-warning option cannot be preserved, the Russian strategic arsenal not only could be decimated by a U.S. strike, but also would depend on the dead hand system of control. Doubts about the resilience of this system persist, however, leading Russian specialists to emphasize the decisive role of the

---

104. Even the newest class of Russian submarines, the Typhoon, is experiencing severe readiness problems. Virtually the entire fleet of Typhoon submarines was undergoing repairs in port in early 1995. Doug Clarke, "Norwegians Say Fire Broke Out on Russian Missile Submarine," *OMRI Daily Digest*, no. 40, pt. 1, February 24, 1995.

nuclear command and control system and the importance of strengthening it.[105] As one expert has said: "The most important priority of the country's military-technology policy should be to preserve and further develop the intelligence, communications, command and control systems of its Strategic Nuclear Forces, as well as the reinstatement [of] its nuclear attack early-warning systems."[106]

To this end the Russians are believed to be building a super-hard, more survivable underground command post in the southern Urals and planning to equip it with a buried low- to extremely low-frequency (LF-ELF) antenna (conceptually similar to the ELF Sanguine program abandoned by the U.S. in favor of a vulnerable ELF Seafarer grid deployed in Wisconsin and Michigan to communicate with deeply submerged U.S. submarines) for disseminating launch orders to Russian missile submarines at sea and SS-25 mobile ICBMs dispersed in the field. Other command bunkers may be under construction in Siberia and elsewhere.

Apart from deficiencies in the command and control system, many Russian observers claim that mobile strategic forces at sea and out of garrison on daily alert, on which Russia would rely for retaliation if circumstances precluded launch on warning by the other strategic forces, are far more vulnerable than is generally believed. American prowess in antisubmarine warfare casts doubt on the wartime longevity of Russian submarines, and a variety of threats against mobile ICBMs have been postulated.

Some of the imagined threats to mobile ICBMs on combat patrol have been overstated. The more alarmist assessments assume that the United States can pinpoint the location and track the movements of all mobile SS-24 and SS-25 missiles dispersed in the field. This alleged capability is attributed to a combination of factors: U.S. space reconnaissance, the intrusive regime of inspection imposed by the START I agreement, and the slowness and route limitations of the truck- and rail-based missiles. These allegations contain some truth. Spy satellites can doubtless locate

105. See Yarynich, "Nuclear Strategies," pp. 10-12.

106. V. N. Tsygichko, "Geopolitical Aspects of Shaping Russia's Nuclear Policy," *Military Thought* (March 3, 1994), p. 8. A similar appeal for strengthening the missile attack early warning system to support launch under attack as well as launch on warning is made by Yarynich, "Nuclear Strategies," p. 11, and by V. F. Grinko and S. I. Kokhan, "Containment and Strategic Stability Concepts under the Contemporary Conditions," *Military Thought* (April 4, 1994), pp. 18-19.

some covertly deployed missiles by using visible light, radar, and infrared detectors, or by monitoring their communications with home base.[107] The verification procedures of START I also require Russia to give the United States access on short notice to as much as 40 percent of the mobile ICBMs in garrison and in the field.[108] Nevertheless, it strains credulity to assert that the United States "has no problem in determining the present location of [Russian] ground-mobile missiles and in forecasting their coordinates in the next 15 minutes."[109]

Having made the crucial assumption that mobile ICBMs cannot be concealed, it is a short leap to posit their devastation by saboteurs, Western aircraft carrying precision-guided conventional munitions, or U.S. submarines.[110] Precision-guided weapons supposedly could be flown undetected through gaps in Russian air defense warning networks to neutralize the mobile strategic forces during a conventional war.[111] As for a nuclear strike by enemy submarines, the mobile missile units, having

107. The deployed SS-25s roam as far as 180 kilometers from their division garrisons and periodically communicate with home base using troposcatter radio links that can be collected by eavesdropping satellites. Other radio channels less susceptible to interception are also used in this activity, however.

108. See particularly sections seven through ten of the "Protocol on Inspections and Continuous Monitoring Activities Relating to the Treaty between the United States of America and the Union of Soviet Socialist Republics on the Reduction and Limitation of Strategic Offensive Arms, " in *Arms Control and Disarmament Agreements: START* (U.S. Arms Control and Disarmament Agency, 1991), pp. 51-60.

109. Colonel Petr Belov, "Who Needs the SS-25 Missiles?" *Segodnya*, March 19, 1994, translated in *JPRS-UMA*, April 27, 1994, pp. 8-9. In another example of this exaggeration, a Russian analyst writes that the "norms of the START I Treaty enable the other side unequivocally to fix the location of each Russian ICBM mobile launcher (land- or railway-based) at any moment." V.S. Stepanov, "On the Destabilizing Factors of Strategic Offensive Arms," *Military Thought* (March 3, 1994), p. 14.

110. Belov, "Who Needs the SS-25 Missiles?" and Stepanov, "On the Destabilizing Factors," develop these attack scenarios in some detail.

111. According to Stepanov, "following the collapse of the USSR, its hitherto smoothly operating air defense system has also been disrupted. . . . The sharp weakening of the air defense system has substantially raised the probability of destruction of Russian mobile ICBM launchers in the event of a conventional war being unleashed by an aggressor both in the state of dispersal and in transit and also during their presence in the limited areas or railway basing points known to the other side." "On the Destabilizing Factors," p. 14.

been previously located, also would presumably fall victim. Some Russian analysts argue that SS-25s could not get outside the lethal radius of U.S. SLBMs during the fifteen-minute flight of the incoming warheads. Petr Belov claims that "calculations show that in this time they will be unable to leave the range of their destruction through shock wave factors."[112]

Claims of mobile ICBM vulnerability have been contested and partially discredited,[113] as have some of their controversial remedial implications such as scrapping the START II Treaty, retaining multiple-warhead missiles in silos, and terminating or drastically scaling back the mobile ICBM program in favor of silo-based ICBMs that supposedly could withstand attack by precision-guided missiles during a prenuclear conflict and launch on warning if nuclear escalation would ensue. The doomsayers have not derailed Russian plans to rely increasingly on mobile ICBMs and submarines and conform to the terms of START II. Although the debate over the treaty and the composition of the future strategic force structure is heating up, Russian plans still call for deploying a single-warhead ICBM force consisting of 540 to 630 mobile SS-25 launchers and 270 to 360 silo launchers,[114] while shifting nearly half their strategic arsenal into submarines.[115] The consensus position presumes that Russia will find the resources necessary to achieve extensive stealth, invulnerability, and combat readiness for a substantial portion of its mobile ICBM and submarine forces.

Nevertheless, the dire forecasts of conservative planners have only been discounted, not rejected out of hand. In particular, the alleged threat

112. Belov, "Who Needs the SS-25 Missiles?" p. 9.

113. An effective rebuttal is Vasiliy Krivokhizha, "Future of the Russian Nuclear Potential," *Rossiyskiye Vesti*, May 11, 1994, in FBIS, *Soviet Union*, May 12, 1994, pp. 27-30.

114. Interview with Lev Volkov, a Russian authority on strategic deployment plans, by Viktor Litovkin, "New Nuclear Missile Program: In 10 Years Russia Will Be Defended by Topols," *Izvestiya*, February 9, 1994, in FBIS, *Soviet Union*, February 9, 1994, p. 4. Volkov estimates that Russia can afford to deploy only 900 ICBMs out of the 1,300 allowed under START II. The upper limit of silo-based ICBMs that he forecasts, 40 percent or 360 ICBMs, suggests that Russia might deploy 105 SS-19 ICBMs (downloaded from six warheads to one) in SS-19 silos, 90 SS-25 ICBMs in SS-18 silos, and 165 SS-25 ICBMs in other silos.

115. The bomber force would carry about 900 warheads, the ICBMs 900, and the submarines 1,650. The submarine force would likely consist of 6 Typhoons (1,200 warheads spread across 120 SLBMs) and 7 Delta IV submarines (448 warheads spread across 112 SLBMs).

posed by conventional forces armed with precision-guided missiles, which American planners have touted, has emerged as a serious theme of Russian strategic planning.[116] Among other effects, this concern produced a rationale for renouncing the no-first-use pledge originally made by the Soviets in 1982.[117] The Russian military doctrine officially adopted in November 1993 indeed dropped the earlier unconditional pledge in favor of a highly qualified policy resembling the U.S. formula.[118] The doctrine implicitly threatens a Russian nuclear response to conventional aggression that covers virtually all prospective adversaries and their allies, including any country that joins NATO.[119] It also specifically notes the likelihood of

116. Classified studies performed in the early 1980s by the U.S. Strategic Air Command showed that conventional weapons, particularly non-nuclear cruise missiles, could contribute substantially to SIOP target coverage, especially targets in poorly defended areas east of the Ural Mountains. In 1991 a study commissioned by SAC and performed by a prominent team of nuclear experts, many of whom hold top positions in the Clinton administration, proposed to add to the SIOP an option to use conventional weapons to attack Russia with "a one-night attack so shocking to the recipient and so indicative of serious U.S. intent that the triggering crisis would be reevaluated in a different light." Thomas C. Reed, "The Role of Nuclear Weapons in the New World Order," briefing for the Joint Strategic Target Planning Staff/Strategic Advisory Group and the Strategic Deterrence Study Group, October 10, 1991, p. 16.

117. This rationale is developed by Grinko and Kokhan, "Containment and Strategic Stability Concepts," pp. 14-21.

118. The doctrine states that "the Russian Federation will not employ its nuclear weapons against any state party to the Treaty on the Nonproliferation of Nuclear Weapons, dated 1 July 1968, which does not possess nuclear weapons except in the cases of: a) an armed attack against the Russian Federation, its territory, Armed Forces, other troops, or its allies by any state which is connected by an alliance agreement with a state that does possess nuclear weapons; b) joint actions by such a state with a state possessing nuclear weapons in the carrying out or in support of any invasion or armed attack upon the Russian Federation, its territory, Armed Forces, other troops, or its allies." "The Basic Provisions of the Military Doctrine of the Russian Federation," *Rossiyskiye Vesti*, November 18, 1993, in FBIS, *Soviet Union*, November 19, 1993, p. 2.

119. For a careful dissection of these nuclear exclusions, see Sergei Rogov, "Russia's New Military Doctrine," *SShA*, no. 4 (1994). A general critique of the nuclear aspects of the doctrine is Alexei Arbatov, "The Nuclear Dilemma of the Military Doctrine: Against Whom Will These Weapons Be Targeted?" *Nezavisimaya Gazeta*, December 3, 1993, in FBIS, *Soviet Union*, December 7, 1993, pp. 27-29.

such escalation if a conventional attack disrupts strategic early warning, command and control, or armed forces.[120]

If U.S. conventional forces have emerged as a salient threat alongside the Trident D-5 force, Russian planners also have to face the distressing prospect of a revived U.S. antiballistic missile program designed to protect American territory. Domestic political support for such a program is on the upswing, to the chagrin of Russia's planners who worry about the implications for their strategic deterrent. Conservative Russian planners could scarcely abide the deployment of antiballistic missile defenses capable of protecting American territory against a ragged retaliatory strike by the few forces surviving a U.S. first strike. Apart from the high attrition of Russian forces that would be suffered during a U.S. nuclear offensive, the coherence of retaliation would suffer if launch control had to devolve to the dead hand system. Under such conditions, an ABM system of even modest configuration, such as one designed to handle a small-scale accidental Russian attack, might be capable of picking off the retaliating Russian missiles. Russian confidence in their deterrent would be dealt another blow.

Russia derives scant reassurance from any part of the U.S. nuclear plan jelling under START II and the nuclear posture review. U.S. deactivation of MX land-based missiles and reduction of warheads on Minuteman III ICBMs from three to one will deflate the counterforce punch of these weapons, but the continuing D-5 deployment on Trident submarines, despite the reduction of each missile's payload from eight to five warheads, will more than offset the loss. Furthermore, the United States plans to retain the capability for redeploying the warheads if political

120. The doctrine states: "Deliberate actions by the aggressor which aim to destroy or disrupt the operation of the strategic nuclear forces, the early-warning system, nuclear power and atomic and chemical industry installations may be factors which increase the danger of a war using conventional weapons escalating into a nuclear war." "Basic Provisions of the Military Doctrine," p. 6. An earlier draft of this doctrine appearing in an influential military journal was unequivocal: "In the course of a war unleashed by an aggressor, his actions involving purposeful disruption of the functioning of strategic nuclear forces and destruction of nuclear power installations and other potentially dangerous installations, including by conventional weapons, will be taken as a transition to the use of weapons of mass destruction." *Military Thought*, May 1992 special edition, in *JPRS-UMT*, June 16, 1992, p. 2.

relations with Russia deteriorate. The NPR bluntly states that the possible emergence of hostile government in Russia calls for a "warhead upload hedge."[121] The United States "must preserve options for uploading/reconstituting U.S. nuclear forces should political relations with Russia change for the worse." This hedge, however prudent it seems to American planners, agitates and worries Russian planners because they see all the hallmarks of a nuclear breakout strategy intended to extend and exploit American nuclear superiority in the crunch. U.S. plans to add warheads will likely enable strategic forces to carry almost twice as many warheads as START II permits; several hundred additional warheads could also be added to nonstrategic nuclear forces.[122]

The potential marginal effect of such reconstitution on the strategic balance is debatable, especially given the protracted timetable for adding most of the SLBM warheads (three months) and ICBM warheads

121. See the NPR briefing released by the Defense Department.
122. The Pentagon envisages, under START II, a nominal strategic nuclear arsenal in 2003 comprising 3,500 warheads carried by 14 Trident submarines (1,680 warheads), 500 Minuteman III ICBMs (500 warheads), and 86 bombers (1,320 warheads). The actual warhead total may be substantially smaller because of fewer bombers and reduced payloads. The air force will be hard pressed to maintain 66 B-52 bombers; 47 is more realistic. Also, the typical bomber payload is 8 to 12 warheads rather than the 16 commonly assumed; this reflects the operational factors that limit the scope of combat missions. In sum, the active bomber force of B-2s and B-52s may carry about 670 warheads and probably no more than 860. Thus the size of the U.S. strategic arsenal as a whole might lie somewhere between 2,850 and 3,040 warheads.

All-out reconstitution of warheads would add another 1,000 to the Minuteman III force, another 1,008 to the Trident submarine fleet, and another 500 to 860 on bombers (depending on the initial peacetime loading, and assuming up to 20 warheads on each of 86 bombers). Assuming a starting inventory of 3,040 warheads, reconstitution would add 2,868, for a total of 5,908. If B-1B bombers now being assigned conventional missions were reconfigured for nuclear missions, more than 1,000 warheads could be added, raising the total to about 7,000, although by early in the next century the depletion of tritium supplies will force cutbacks in nuclear stockpiles and effectively preclude keeping such sizable numbers of reserve warheads for B-1B bombers. If nuclear-armed Tomahawk sea-launched cruise missiles were also redeployed on attack submarines and surface ships during a crisis, another 400 warheads would join the inventory, for a grand total of 7,400 nuclear warheads. A more realistic estimate, given tritium shortfalls and other constraints, is 6,000.

(eighteen months).[123] The Clinton administration's mere contemplation of a doubling of deliverable U.S. strategic warheads nonetheless bruises Russian sensibilities. In their view the warhead upload hedge, however long it would take to implement, makes a mockery of post–cold war nuclear rapprochement.

The effect of the hedge on safety is less debatable. Russia will almost certainly imitate the American plan, resulting in much greater dispersion of Russian reserve nuclear weapons than would otherwise occur, which in turn will make safety and security all the more difficult to maintain.

The overall effect of U.S. nuclear plans on the safety of Russian nuclear operations is no less harmful. U.S. strategic forces increasingly threaten all Russian nuclear forces and command and control functions with sudden destruction. Deployment of Russian forces in vulnerable silos is being abandoned, even though their safeguards are the strongest, in favor of mobile ICBM and submarine deployments with weaker safeguards. The mobile as well as silo-based strategic forces and their command and control effectiveness depend more heavily than ever on launch on warning and the dead hand system, neither of which appear to be reliable in underwriting either deterrence or safety. Russia's strategic difficulties, while substantially self-inflicted, pose safety problems that the United States is unwittingly doing more to exacerbate than relieve.

The underlying U.S. threat perceived by Russian planners is of course not intended to be that of a first strike. U.S. planners define the strategic doctrine of the United States to be deterrence based on the threat of retaliation, not preemption. Russian assessment of its vulnerability nonetheless assumes U.S. initiation of a maximum attack because that

123. In an emergency the U.S. Navy could load reserve warheads on to D-5 missiles at a rate of 40 a week; the entire reserve inventory of 1,008 warheads could be loaded in about six months. The air force could load reserve warheads on Minuteman III missiles at a rate of about 6 or 7 a week; the entire reserve inventory could be loaded in three years. The air force could put on alert and arm the B-52 and B-2 bomber force with a full complement of active and reserve warheads (a maximum of 1,720) in a matter of weeks. The time needed to load nuclear arms on B-1B bombers previously converted for conventional missions would be very long, as would the time for reconfiguring aircraft carriers to conduct nuclear missions. It could take several years to complete the nuclear rearmament of aircraft carriers. By contrast, the redeployment of nuclear-tipped sea-launched cruise missiles on attack submarines would probably take only a few weeks to complete.

capability exists. This assumption follows the conservative tradition of cold war analysis using standard technical calculations. The retaliatory character of U.S. strategy, not to mention the absence of any U.S. motive to initiate an attack, do not figure into such calculations. Worst-case analysis of this sort severely distorts the strategic situation, but it shapes Russian perceptions just the same.

America's Unstable Nuclear Posture

The U.S. nuclear posture is not immune to similar operational difficulties. Although it is stable relative to Russia's and to what it was in the past, it has some unstable facets that the next decade will only make worse. Under START II constraints and NPR guidance, there could easily be greater operational instability in 2003 than today. The charted course will reinforce the U.S. dependence on launch on warning and incur other safety risks.

AMERICA'S TARGETING CULTURE. The operational disposition of U.S. strategic forces embodies a single-minded pursuit: covering targets in the former Soviet Union. The overriding goal of strategic planning is to ensure that U.S. strategic forces can destroy virtually all of the targets in four major categories: nuclear forces, other military forces, the military-industrial sector, and civilian and military leadership. Blanket coverage must be ensured under a range of stressful wartime conditions, including a surprise preemptive strike by Russian strategic forces. The extent of the target coverage that strategic organizations expect to achieve, damage expectancy expressed in its simplest form as the percentage of the target base that would be destroyed in retaliation, varies under these conditions. Strategic planners strive to ensure that damage expectancy would approach 100 percent, although 70 to 90 percent would generally meet the minimum essential requirement in the various target categories.

The demands of target coverage or damage expectancy determine the alert status, target assignments, and launch response times of U.S. strategic forces. These norms are key to understanding the American nuclear universe and its hidden safety hazards. Among other roles, they powerfully shape the operational predilections of the U.S. command system—for instance, its predisposition to launch on warning instead of launching after an attack is ridden out and its readiness to delegate launch authority down the chain of command beforehand.

During the cold war, damage expectancy requirements disposed strategic commanders to raise the alert level of the whole nuclear arsenal in a crisis, to rely on launch on warning in wartime, and to assume predelegated authority to launch the forces if presidential direction were disrupted. These actions, all of which would have compromised safety, flowed from the requirement to be ready and able to destroy a huge number of Soviet targets. In 1986, for example, SIOP forces were assigned 16,000 individual Soviet targets. To even begin to cover this enormous number, the entire U.S. strategic arsenal of 11,000 warheads would have been pressed into service. All forces would have needed to be brought to alert, and all would have had to be launched before they or their command system suffered losses from a Soviet strike. Even then, the maximum damage that could have been achieved if every U.S. bomber, submarine, and ICBM survived and delivered its full payload to its intended targets would have fallen short of the damage expectancy requirements. In the best case the damage expectancy could not have exceeded about 70 percent.

Today, damage expectancy norms put less strain on nuclear posture, but this condition is temporary; it reflects a large and rapid contraction of the target base owing to the dissolution of the Soviet empire and a smaller and slower contraction of the U.S. strategic arsenal. The target base has shrunk from 16,000 in 1985 to 2,500 in 1995, a decrease of 84 percent, but the U.S. active inventory of strategic warheads has dropped from 11,000 in 1985 to 7,800 in 1995, a decrease of only 29 percent.[124] The decline in the number of targets has been nearly three times greater than the reduction in weapons available to attack the targets.

This weapons-rich situation is unique and should allow for some lowering of alert levels and reduced reliance on both launch on warning and nuclear predelegation. (The surfeit of weapons also presents an opportunity to assign them to third world targets.) The nuclear posture review did consider eliminating launch on warning from the repertoire of current options and adopting a strategy of delayed retaliation, but this proposal was decisively rejected, presumably in part because calculations of target coverage by current and future strategic forces show that launch on warning is necessary to achieve high damage expectancy.

124. Another 800 or so targets in China, North Korea, Iran, and elsewhere, the vast majority of which are in China, are listed on the target base for the U.S. strategic reserve force. The 2,500 targets mentioned are covered by strategic forces assigned to the single integrated operational plan.

Current forces on daily alert could ride out an attack and, assuming survivable command and control, still destroy 65 percent of the target base.[125] But that performance, relying entirely on nuclear-arms submarines, falls short of requirements. If the MX and Minuteman III ICBM force were launched before incoming Soviet warheads could hit them, the strategic commanders could achieve a damage expectancy of 100 percent and still have a reserve force of 700 warheads on withheld submarines.[126] In the more plausible circumstance of a Russian attack during a nuclear crisis in which available U.S. submarines (those not in overhaul) have surged out of port, current U.S. forces could ride out an attack before retaliating and still destroy 83 percent of the targets.[127] In this circumstance, launch on warning would be unnecessary, especially if strategic bombers could be reconstituted as a reserve force.

The weapons-rich situation that allows some leeway for relaxing the nuclear hair trigger is ephemeral, however. Although the target base should shrink somewhat (to perhaps 2,000 from 2,500), the number of weapons available to cover the targets will decrease faster (to 3,500 from 7,800). Calculations show that in conforming to the NPR blueprint and the terms of START II, the U.S. posture will be subjected once again to acute pressures to launch on warning to ensure target coverage. The stressful conditions of the cold war will return in that damage expectancy norms will require the alerting of all nuclear weapons during a crisis and their quick launch in the event of a Russian attack. If U.S. forces on day-to-day alert do not launch

125. This estimate assumes that the off-alert bomber force is destroyed along with the alert ICBM force. It assumes that out of the 2,880 warheads in the submarine force, 70 percent are at sea and are survivable; that the overall reliability of SLBMs is 80 percent; and that a delivered SLBM warhead destroys its target. Under these assumptions, the 1995 submarine force could deliver 1,613 warheads and destroy 65 percent of the 2,500 targets.

126. This estimate derives from the combination of 1,613 warheads delivered by submarines and 1,588 warheads delivered by ICBMs, a total of 3,201. It assumes that out of 2,090 ICBM warheads in the arsenal, 95 percent are available for prompt launch, that the available warheads have an overall reliability of 80 percent, and that a delivered ICBM warhead destroys its target.

127. This estimate assumes that 90 percent of the submarine force can be deployed at sea during a crisis. This alert rate (up from the 70 percent rate assumed for daily peacetime conditions) would result in 2,074 deliverable warheads that would destroy 83 percent of the 2,500 target base (assuming reliability is 80 percent and each delivered warhead destroys its target).

on warning, only 47 percent of the target base would be destroyed.[128] And even if ICBMs launch on warning, the damage expectancy, 66 percent, would still be unacceptable to military planners.[129] Thus the U.S. posture will also depend on the alerting of off-alert forces, particularly submarines. After being generated in a crisis, the submarine force alone could destroy 61 percent of the targets.[130] Together with ICBMs launched on warning, the combined forces could destroy 80 percent.[131] And together with the bomber force, the triad, if launched on warning, could destroy 100 percent and still keep 450 weapons in reserve.[132]

It scarcely seems possible that such theoretical calculations would continue to be critically important to strategic planners in the years

128. This estimate assumes that the off-alert bomber force and the alert ICBM force are destroyed. The latter assumption is debatable because of the uncertain accuracy of the SS-25 missiles available for use in 2003. The estimate also assumes that out of 1,680 warheads in the submarine force, 70 percent are deployed at sea and are survivable, that the SLBMs have an overall reliability of 80 percent, and that a delivered warhead would destroy its target. Under these assumptions, 941 SLBM warheads would destroy 47 percent of 2,000 targets.

129. This estimate combines the 941 warheads delivered by SLBMs with 380 warheads delivered by ICBMs. This assumes that out of 500 warheads in the ICBM arsenal (500 single-warhead Minuteman IIIs), 95 percent are alert and available for prompt launch, that the overall reliability of available ICBMs is 80 percent, and that a delivered ICBM warhead would destroy its target. A total of 1,321 warheads would destroy 66 percent of 2,000 targets.

130. This estimate assumes that 90 percent of the 1,680 warheads in the submarine arsenal are deployed at sea and survivable under crisis conditions and that the reliability of SLBMs is 80 percent. The submarine force thus delivers 1,210 warheads against 2,000 targets for a damage expectancy of 61 percent. All off-alert U.S. bombers and alert ICBMs are assumed to be destroyed.

131. This estimate combines the 1,210 delivered SLBM warheads with 380 delivered ICBM warheads (the latter figure derived from a 95 percent alert rate and 80 percent reliability rate for a 500-warhead ICBM force in 2003). The total number of delivered warheads would be 1,590, which would destroy 80 percent of 2,000 targets.

132. This estimate combines 1,210 SLBM warheads, 380 ICBM warheads, and 864 bomber warheads. The bomber estimate assumes that out of a total of 1,350 warheads in the bomber arsenal in 2003, 80 percent would be put on runway alert in a crisis, that the alert bomber force has an overall reliability of 80 percent, and that a delivered bomber warhead would destroy its target. A total of 2,454 warheads would be deliverable; 2,000 would be used to destroy 100 percent of 2,000 targets, and 454 would be held in reserve.

ahead. Assessments of this kind strike the ordinary observer as throwbacks to the cold war, vestiges of nuclear warfighting models that drove strategic programs during the nadir of U.S.-Russian relations. A new framework for the post–cold war era, based on other principles of nuclear security, could surely compete with one based almost exclusively on principles of rapid annihilation of thousands of targets in the former Soviet Union. Nonetheless, the old framework has not been replaced. It still strongly shapes the strategic war plan. A targeting mania permeates the culture of strategic organizations to an extent that is hard to overemphasize.

NPR: BUSINESS AS USUAL. The old habits of mind and organization thwart efforts to recast the nuclear posture. The nuclear posture review failed miserably in this regard. In the end it endorsed the status quo and preserved the cold war culture of obsessive targeting. Certain basic features of the posture seem immutable. Rapid reaction is one of them. Another is inflexibility. The NPR reaffirmed, for instance, a time-honored constraint on the choice of options in the strategic war plan: the minimum SIOP attack in the event of war with Russia requires a comprehensive assault on Russia's nuclear forces and support bases. This represents the largest target category, perhaps 50 percent of the target base. Any major attack option directed at the other smaller target categories would automatically unleash an attack on Russian nuclear forces.

To the extent that flexibility has been increased, it has taken the form of "withholds" (now called add-ons) that allow decisionmakers to exclude certain countries such as Ukraine, Belarus, and Kazakhstan from some of the major attack plans. Advances in adaptive planning also enable Strategic Command to readily modify the latest single integrated operational plan (a SIOP 94 should have gone into effect about September 1994) to enable strikes against selected subsets of Russian strategic forces that may fall under the control of renegade local commanders—for instance, a rebel commander and staff of a division of strategic rockets.[133]

133. Speculation along these lines is stimulated by the history of the latest SIOP. It grew out of the president's nuclear initiative in late 1991 which took many U.S. strategic and tactical nuclear weapons off alert in the wake of the August 1991 coup in Moscow. This initiative led to a new nuclear weapons employment policy (NUWEP) from the secretary of defense in 1992, a time when nuclear anarchy in the FSU was widely viewed as the predominant nuclear threat. This NUWEP directed

Such special options would borrow the approach taken to general nuclear war and apply it to the case of a breakdown of nuclear control. It would reflect the popular but misguided view that strategic targeting offers a solution to the problem of nuclear anarchy.

Another continuing feature of the U.S. nuclear posture is decentralization. The NPR apparently did not challenge the tradition of predelegating nuclear launch authority to senior military commanders designated as prepositioned national command authorities or propose tightening central control over other nuclear activities such as crisis alerting. Predelegation was practiced throughout the cold war, at least until the mid-1980s, and perhaps remains in effect, an arrangement that has entailed the widespread physical distribution of authorization and unlock codes (recall the incident in which the unlock codes were compromised on board a strategic command airborne command post).[134] The arrangement also entailed giving the designated military commanders the right to order the implementation of the strategic war plan promptly in the event of a confirmed nuclear attack that disrupts communications and isolates the strategic forces from the president and others in the chain of presidential succession. (The preconditions for exercising this launch authority—verified nuclear detonations and communications outage—are the same conditions that activate the Russian dead hand system.) A case can be made for revoking such arrangements on the grounds that safety takes precedence over the demands of targeting. An unconditional revocation, however, would change the basic character of the U.S. nuclear posture. It would be resisted no less strongly than attempts to promote

the Joint Chiefs of Staff to develop new guidance for Strategic Command, guidance that would have come out in the usual form of a joint strategic capabilities plan. The plan's specific instructions in annex C would have provided the basis for building a new SIOP, which should have gone into effect in 1994 because the time between the issuance of a new NUWEP and the programming of a new operational SIOP is normally two years. Given the continuing concern over the control of Russian and Ukrainian nuclear weapons, it would be surprising if these documents did not require some SIOP adjustments to deal with threats of nuclear anarchy. Incidentally, given the multiyear lag time for generating a new SIOP, the next SIOP reflecting the September 1994 nuclear posture review should not be finished and go into effect until 1997.

134. For more information on nuclear predelegation during the cold war, see Blair, *Logic of Accidental Nuclear War*, especially pp. 46-50.

safety through such other means as eliminating the option to launch on warning.

Relaxing the Nuclear Postures: Options for Dealerting

In the post–cold war era, when nuclear command and control in Russia is shaky, providence in nuclear planning requires major departures, however controversial, from current policy and operational practices. Principles of nuclear security need to be reformulated with a view to adjusting the current balance between the goals of deterrence and safety. The guiding principles should ensure that the safety of nuclear weapons is ironclad, nuclear postures are incapable of mounting a sudden massive and deliberate strike, nuclear forces are afforded reliable and timely strategic early warning if an opponent prepares offensive nuclear weapons for attack, the postures do not depend on tactical warning for their survival, and the posture support delayed, rather than prompt, retaliation.

Various possible options alter the nuclear postures to conform, in different degrees, with these principles. Four of these, and their variants, are described and evaluated in the following discussion.

Detargeting Land-Based Missiles

In the afterglow of the Vancouver summit in early 1993 between Presidents Clinton and Yeltsin, the White House announced that the United States had begun "a comprehensive review of measures that could enhance strategic stability, including the possibility of each side reprogramming its nuclear missiles so they are not routinely aimed at each other."[135] By late 1993 the Defense Department and strategic command had closely examined the idea of detargeting and prepared an option called broad ocean area targeting for consideration by President Clinton.[136] An agreement was struck at the Clinton-Yeltsin summit in January 1994 to implement such a plan by May 30, 1994.

The paucity of information about Russian targeting procedures and

135. "Statement by the President on Advancing U.S. Relations with Russia and the other New Independent States," Office of the Press Secretary, the White House, April 23, 1993, p. 1.
136. Michael R. Gordon with Eric Schmitt, "U.S. Is Considering Aiming Its Missiles away from Russia," *New York Times*, December 6, 1993, p. A1.

capabilities requires this discussion to focus on U.S. practices. The two systems, however, are probably similar enough that the U.S. system can illustrate the detargeting possibilities on both sides. Considering the current and near-term configuration of the command and control systems for U.S. strategic missiles, two detargeting schemes for U.S. land-based forces can be readily distinguished.

BROAD OCEAN AREA TARGETING. The easiest approach, and the one already implemented by the United States and Russia (subsequently joined by Britain and China), is to aim missiles away from their wartime targets and point them at the ocean. This approach applies to strategic missiles that must have target data in their computer memory to maintain launch readiness: the U.S. Minuteman III and older classes of Russian ICBMs. The MX Peacekeeper missiles and U.S. and Russian submarine-launched ballistic missiles as well as some of the newest classes of Russian ICBMs do not normally hold target data even when they maintain a high level of launch readiness. Thus this plan does not affect them except, presumably, during periodic weapons system checkouts and launch countdown exercises.

For Minuteman III, Russia has become a reserve target instead of the primary target. Each missile has been programmed with a non-Russian primary target, which could be a nominal target such as a point in the ocean. The detargeting commitment also extends to all other previously targeted states in the former Soviet Union and elsewhere.

The programming of a new primary target in each missile has been carried out by strategic command headquarters and ICBM launch control centers in the field.[137] Within twenty-five hours of round-the-clock reprogramming using established procedures, all Minuteman III missiles

137. The procedure would entail having the strategic command calculate and transmit new primary target information for each affected missile and its warheads (currently up to 500 Minuteman III missiles armed with 1,500 warheads) to the associated launch control center (one for each 10 missiles) in the field through the SACDIN communications network. The launch crew would then record the new data into its computer hard drive (magnetic control group). Alternatively, strategic command could send the new primary target information to the codes division at each missile base, which would then dispatch special targeting teams to the launch control center to load up the computers.

In either case each Minuteman III launch center (MX is a different story) then would have to transfer the targeting data from its computer to the 10 missiles in its flight. This transfer via underground cable and medium-frequency radio would be accomplished by a computer command known as remote data change (T), which is a

could have been set on nominal primary targets with Russian and other specific wartime targets transferred into the missiles' reserve target set.[138] It was technically possible to reduce this time to nine hours by altering the computer time-sharing schedule among the five launch centers in any given Minuteman III squadron, but this would have been highly irregular and might have delayed instead of expedited the reprogramming. A new program called rapid execution and combat targeting is being implemented in 1995 to enable the centers to program new targets in a third less time than has been the case.

Having been retargeted in this manner, the entire Minuteman III force was aimed at the oceans but also programmed to allow for quickly restoring Russia as the primary target under crisis or wartime conditions. A single computer command (called a positive-control launch A command) issued by the underground or airborne launch control centers on orders from higher authority could instruct all the Minuteman III missiles to aim at targets in Russia. The command entails dialing two digits into a device and turning a switch for a few seconds, initiating an automated process known as realignment in which all the missiles are simultaneously retargeted within seconds to as much as twenty minutes, at which time they could be launched.[139] The strategic war plans (SIOP

component of the command data buffer system in the center. The 1970s-vintage computer time-sharing arrangement, computer capacity (only 64K), and cable limitations within each squadron (a squadron consists of 5 launch control centers and 50 missiles), allow only 1 missile to be retargeted at a time in each squadron, which takes 30 minutes to complete. Since there are 10 active Minuteman III ICBM squadrons, and 500 missiles, it would take 25 hours to reprogram the entire force. This estimate is somewhat longer than the air force estimate of 20.5 hours.

138. A Minuteman III missile has four target sets in its missile guidance computer. Each set contains target data for all three warheads carried by the missile. Three of the sets are reserve targets. Thus a missile could have three distinct Russian (or other country) target sets in reserve.

139. Actual times depend on whether the retargeting mode is minimum reaction time (MRT) or circular error probable (CEP). In the very fast MRT mode, the wartime target and the peacetime ocean target both lie within a certain small azimuth angle from the launch point, and the missile can perform its realignment after launch mainly by adjusting the elevation angle of its trajectory. In the CEP mode, the cold war target lies outside the azimuth flexibility of a missile aimed at the ocean, and the missile must therefore realign its guidance platform before launch. This realignment would typically take fifteen to thirty minutes to complete.

options) undoubtedly allow the vast majority of the missiles to be retargeted in seconds rather than minutes. This rapid reversal allegedly ensures that the U.S. missile force could still be fired before Russian missiles could attack them.

This emergency procedure for reaiming the missile force at Russia or another country targeted in the strategic war plan can be carried out in conjunction with increasing the alert status of forces during a crisis or with ordering the launch of the forces in wartime. If the United States plans to preserve its option to launch on warning, the Minuteman III retargeting must either be accomplished during the crisis preceding any Russian attack or the missiles must be aimed in peacetime at ocean targets that lie on the line of the missiles' Russian target trajectories. By aiming the missiles at the Arctic Ocean in peacetime, the switch to Russian targets does not require an azimuth realignment in the silos, and the target switch is virtually instantaneous with trajectory modifications made in flight.

If tradition is a reliable guide, however, retargeting will be undertaken as part of an increase in the defense readiness condition of U.S. nuclear forces during a crisis. Retargeting will likely become a standard operating procedure of nuclear crisis alert. Tradition would also support a provision that would allow the strategic command headquarters to issue the retargeting order, if it had not done so already, to all forces as soon as it received positive indications of a Russian missile attack from the early warning network. This order would initiate the missile realignment process before the national command authorities were even notified of an attack. An early start on retargeting would be essential to preserve the option of launch on warning for any Minuteman III missiles that require a lengthy (twenty minute) azimuth realignment before launch. If the launch crews had to wait for the president to render a launch decision and for the launch order to arrive before initiating the retargeting process, those missiles could not be launched before incoming Russian warheads arrived.

Even with the head start, missiles that require lengthy realignment time in their silos (undoubtedly a small fraction of the force) would at best barely beat the deadline under conditions of Russian missile attack. The time required to detect an attack, realign the missiles, and complete the launch procedures, plus an additional few minutes of fly-out time, would likely exceed the thirty-minute flight time of incoming Russian ICBMs. The U.S. missiles thus might fail to launch in time to escape damage or destruction. Moreover, the first nuclear explosion to occur in the missile fields would shake the ground so vigorously that unlaunched missiles could be knocked out of alignment, forcing them to repeat the realignment procedure and thereby leaving them vulnerable to subsequent missile strikes.[140]

This tight constraint on reaction time puts a premium on retargeting at an early stage of a crisis. But to take the step then could be provocative and aggravate crisis tensions, defeating one of the main objectives of the detargeting idea: providing mutual reassurance that nuclear intentions are not aggressive. The procedure could be carried out in secrecy in the hope that it would escape Russia's notice. But inasmuch as emergency retargeting would likely be performed as a standard procedure during any increase in the defense readiness level, and because Russia almost certainly would hear the order for, and detect the change in, the overall alert level of U.S. forces, it would not be fooled. Yet this step might be taken without the knowledge and careful consideration of U.S. political authorities if it were just another item on the alert checklist. Crisis management could become complicated if the step were ordered by the U.S. military at the wrong time under the wrong circumstances for the sake of expediting preparations for retaliation or projecting a greater deterrent threat.

The safety of nuclear operations should be slightly improved by the detargeting scheme the United States and Russia have adopted. An accidentally launched Minuteman III missile flying under normal power and guidance would fall short of its cold war target in Russia and land instead in the Arctic Ocean. The obvious question is why did the nuclear superpowers not adopt this safety measure much earlier? Its value during the height of the cold war would have been greater, given the stronger probability that an accidental nuclear missile strike would have sparked a general nuclear exchange. And its adoption would have incurred no risk to deterrence, given the ease and speed with which it can be reversed.

This ease of reversal means that it scarcely relaxes the hair trigger on the operational postures. It seems ironic, in fact, that proponents of this detargeting option tout its rapid reversibility as one of its main virtues, when the imperative of speed is and will continue to be the primary safety

---

140. Motion sensors in the silos are supposed to freeze the guidance system to prevent this lengthy realignment, though at minimum some recalibration would need to be performed by the missile guidance computer.

hazard. They have misdiagnosed the problem and contrived a remedy that fails to treat the main source of danger. Broad ocean area targeting does nothing at all to strengthen safeguards against inadvertent or unauthorized launches aided and abetted by rapid reaction postures. Even if all missiles designated for launch could instantaneously switch from ocean aimpoints to targets in Russia, launch on warning allows a president only five to ten minutes to consult with advisors and reach a decision to launch. Under this hasty and rigid timeline, a nuclear war could plausibly begin in error. Moreover, if the attack were real, the slightest delay could result in most friendly forces being destroyed before or after liftoff. Last, the targeting does not hinder initiating a sudden attack. It is misleading to suggest that the end of the cold war has permitted the traditional adversaries to institute less aggressive targeting practices. They may have taken a symbolic step toward that end, but as a practical matter the detargeting plan has a trivial impact on the readiness of the strategic forces to launch preemptively as well as to launch on warning.

Launch on warning is fraught with risk. By risking an inadvertent launch triggered by false warning while making the survival of land-based missiles in a real attack precarious, launch on warning puts enormous pressures on commanders at all levels. Yet both sides remain committed to nuclear strategies geared to beating a thirty-minute launch deadline. For the United States, such rapid reaction is necessary to meet the excessive demands for target coverage imposed by presidential guidance currently in effect (national security decision directive 13 signed by President Reagan in 1981, as modified or supplemented by President Clinton's endorsement of the nuclear posture review). The rapid reversibility of the targeting is thus no virtue because the underlying requirement is inherently dangerous.

Some Russian nuclear planners have disparaged the agreement for additional reasons: its unverifiability and its onerous burden of implementation. Their compliance with broad ocean area targeting has involved more cumbersome retargeting procedures for their older ICBMs, particularly any SS-13s and SS-11s that may remain in their inventory. Whereas the United States has performed the procedures by remote retargeting from the launch control centers, the Russians probably have had to dispatch targeting teams to the individual silos to load up Arctic targets into the computers of older systems. This process is managed by the command posts of their missile divisions and is labor intensive. Also, the centralized nature of the Russian nuclear command system means that the entire chain of nuclear command has to work out new responsibilities and procedures to implement the plan. For the older missiles that require labor-intensive retargeting, the option of launch on warning cannot be exercised unless the wartime targets are restored during a nuclear crisis.

Newer classes of Russian ICBMs, notably SS-24s and SS-25s, and perhaps one or more classes of the fourth-generation missiles (SS-17, SS-18, and SS-19), apparently do not hold targeting data in missile memory during normal peacetime alert. Like that for the U.S. MX, the data reside outside the missile; in the case of the MX, the data are kept in a computer rack in the silo and fed into the missile on orders from launch control centers just before launch. These classes of missiles thus fall outside the scope of ocean retargeting, and those maintained on full alert should be able to be launched quickly at any time.

COMPREHENSIVE DETARGETING. An alternative to ocean targeting is comprehensive detargeting. This approach assumes that the nuclear superpowers should be striving to eliminate, not preserve, their reliance on quick-launch tactics.

A serious plan for detargeting would strip the targets from every ICBM missile's memory or keep only nominal targets like the oceans. The command systems would then lose their ability to fire first quickly or to launch on warning using land-based missiles. The U.S. command system would take thirty to forty-five minutes to retarget 10 Minuteman III ICBMs (out of a total of 500 in the force); it would take twenty-five hours to retarget the entire Minuteman force using procedures described earlier. Only underground launch centers can perform these procedures; airborne launch centers are not equipped for them.

Comprehensive detargeting requires the deletion of targets from the computer hard drives in the Minuteman III and MX underground launch control centers, as well as the targeting computers inside MX silos. This would extend the crisis or wartime retargeting time even more for Minuteman III. It would also impose a significant constraint on MX targeting. MX missiles, slated for elimination under START II, do not normally carry targets in their missile memory. Wartime targets are loaded into them as part of their quick-launch procedures, and missile alignment occurs in flight using astral references. To deprive this particular force of a quick-launch capability, the target information must be removed from local launch control centers and silo computers.

The combination of these measures would deprive the United States of its ability to launch any ICBMs in retaliation except on a delayed schedule. If the measures were reciprocal and verifiable, however, the issue would be moot because the Russian missile force could not mount a sudden attack in the first place.

Russian reciprocation would require the elimination of targeting data from the regimental command posts of all ICBM classes, especially SS-24s and SS-25s. Higher command posts capable of loading preset target data would also have to relinquish their data.

VERIFICATION. This detargeting plan for Minuteman III and MX missiles as well as some classes of Russian missiles could be monitored and verified by intrusive means. The newer Russian missiles, however, pose more difficult if not intractable problems for verification and perhaps would need to be dealerted by other means.

On the U.S. side, the basic idea is to designate one of the five redundant launch control centers in each missile squadron as an inspection and monitoring station. This center would be defanged; all the war plan documentation would be removed, and the launch, enable, and inhibit codes would be eliminated from the electronic panels.

A joint U.S.-Russian team (two two-person crews) would inhabit the center, with teams rotating so as to maintain continuous monitoring. The Russian teams would receive the same basic training provided to U.S. launch control officers at Vandenburg Air Force Base except for the procedures known as emergency war orders. The Russians would learn everything necessary to perform monitoring duties at the designated center in the field.

From this center, the team could fully monitor the status of every missile in the fifty-missile squadron. The members could at any time interrogate every missile by computer to check its target status, and they would automatically receive computer reports from every missile whose status changed as a result of commands issued by the other four launch centers in the squadron. In the event of a deliberate effort by the combat crews in the other centers to insert new targets (which, as the Russian team would understand from their extensive training and field experience, is the only means to retarget the missiles), the monitoring team would be instantly alerted by reports from the missiles.

The joint teams could also conduct quick inspections of the combat launch centers for Minuteman III and MX to request a case input printout that would reveal the geographic coordinates of any and all targets stored in the center's computer; the printout should be empty or hold coordinates for ocean targets, depending on the targeting agreement. MX silos could also be inspected to ensure that no targeting data are present in the computer rack in the equipment room.

Violations of these detargeting provisions could be reported within minutes to the proper authorities on either side via dedicated communications links. Although the configuration of these on-line channels lies beyond the scope of this analysis, they could be installed at modest expense, and reliably effective and timely procedures for clarifying the cause of any outage on them could be established.

As an incidental but important benefit, the links could be used by the team to augment the Russian missile attack early warning system. In the event of a false warning from Russian tactical warning sensors, the teams could quickly provide reassurance to the proper authorities (in this case, the Russian early warning center and the general staff in particular) that U.S. strategic missiles had not been launched.

Continuous monitoring of all U.S. ICBM forces allowed under START II (500 Minuteman III missiles each with a single warhead) would require that a joint team serve around the clock in each of ten centers, one for each of the ten missile squadrons spread across several bases in the western United States. Ten joint teams thus serve simultaneously, requiring at least another ten to provide for relief and time off.

A similar arrangement would be established in Russia. Joint teams would be trained and assigned to launch centers throughout the country and provided with the appropriate report channels to NORAD and the Pentagon. Russia also has redundant launch centers, not only at the regimental level but also at higher levels (especially the division level), that could probably support this function adequately. Indeed, the Russian ICBM control system for silo-based forces is far more elaborate and centralized than its U.S. counterpart. Unlike U.S. land-based missiles, Russian missiles in silos continuously and automatically report their status to the highest levels of the nuclear command chain in Moscow. (U.S. missile squadrons are islands electronically isolated from higher levels.) Joint monitoring teams could thus occupy positions at several levels in the nuclear command hierarchy.

Detargeting Submarine-Launched Missiles

Missiles on board alert U.S. strategic submarines are normally dormant except for brief periods during weapons system checks; the target information resides in a disk drive apart from the missiles. There it remains until the crew receives launch orders. Then the crew accelerates the gyroscopes and inserts the target data into the missile guidance, a process requiring about ten minutes. If the orders call for strikes against new targets that had not been prestored in the disk drive, the crew requires substantially more time to convert the new target coordinates into target instructions that can be fed into the missile guidance. This computational process can be shortened somewhat if the new targets have been listed already in target books (but not preprogrammed in the disk drive). One or two hours is required to reprogram the missiles to strike altogether new target coordinates.

Detargeting, strictly defined, is therefore not a meaningful option for U.S. submarines. Even if all target data were erased from the disk drive, the SSBN possesses the inherent capacity to generate targeting data and load it into the missile guidance set. By contrast, Russian submarines appear to be sharply limited in this respect. They rely on preprogrammed targeting tapes provided before leaving port, without which targeting and launch could not be performed.

Detargeting, more broadly defined, could mean that submarines would stay out of range of targets during their patrols. For U.S. Trident submarines with missile warheads reduced from eight to five as planned, which increases the D-5 missile range by more than one-third, major portions of Russia could be struck from the moment a submarine leaves port. This makes it infeasible to operate Tridents based at either the Atlantic or Pacific home ports out of range of major targets. Russian SSBNs would have even less latitude to operate out of range, given the location of their northern and eastern ports and their reliance on protection by friendly forces in home waters against intrusions of Western antisubmarine warfare forces.

Modest Dealerting Measures for ICBMs and SSBNs

Additional steps could be taken to dealert ICBMs. One measure is to "safe" the missiles in their unmanned silos, as was done to the 450 Minuteman II missiles in October 1991 as part of President Bush's unilateral move to reduce nuclear alert rates. Maintenance crews enter each silo and insert a special pin into the motor ignition mechanism. This physically blocks ignition. To reverse the procedure, the crews have to return to each silo and pull the pin, a more time-consuming procedure than might be expected. The Russians surely have a comparable option for their silo-based ICBMs that is equally time-consuming to reverse.

A more effective measure of slowing reaction times for most classes of ICBMs, including all U.S. and Russian silo-based missiles, would be to shut off power to the missiles, which would take a very long time to reverse. Maintenance crews would have to go to each silo and perform a long checklist of procedures to restore power to the launch equipment and missile subsystems. This elaborate task involves a sequence of checks to ensure that each subsystem is properly functioning. Then the on-site crew throws a switch that transfers full monitoring and launch control to the parent launch control center in the flight. The launch crew then performs a set of procedures to load targeting data into the missile guidance system and verify the correctness of the data.

For the U.S. force as a whole, and probably the Russian force as well, it would take three to four days to restore power even under emergency maintenance schedules. A major liability of this measure, however, is that the delicate guidance sets on the missiles are prone to malfunction when spun up as power is restored. This deficiency could be eliminated if new guidance systems were built so that land-based missiles could lapse into a dormant state like the SLBMs.[141] Another liability, which especially applies to Russian ICBMs, is that self-diagnostic instruments and environmental controls that improve safety would be adversely affected.

The joint teams discussed earlier could conduct challenge on-site inspections of U.S. missile silos to ensure that the missiles remained without power and safed by the motor pins. This check would be simplified by the fact that restoring power and ignition capability to missiles would require maintenance teams to enter each silo. The monitoring center would be notified whenever any maintenance crew (or anybody else) entered any silo in the squadron. Outer and inner zone security alerts would be automatically reported to the center in such cases, identifying the best candidates for challenge on-site inspections.

The reaction times of submarines could also be substantially slowed if their crews would refrain from performing the complex and time-consuming procedures required to prepare their missiles for rapid launch. A U.S. submarine's reaction time could be lengthened from fifteen minutes or so to eighteen hours. U.S. SSBNs take at least that long after leaving

141. Such a program exists but is not funded. It is called the guidance replacement program phase II. The effect of the program on regeneration time is unclear; it may provide for reconstitution that would be too fast.

port to complete the procedures—for instance, the removal of flood plates from the launch tubes and weapons systems checkout—that enable them to assume a launch-ready disposition. Russian submarines doubtless undergo similar preparations before assuming full combat alert. It would be difficult to verify that the preparations were not made, however, and therefore unusual monitoring arrangements would have to be devised.

The at-sea alert rate of strategic submarines could be cut as part of a dealerting policy. For the United States, cutting back to a single-crew concept, which the Russians have always used, and operating the SSBNs in the way U.S. attack submarines (SSNs) are operated (making numerous port calls), would reduce the time spent at sea from eight months to four months a year. This halving of the alert rate, reducing the fraction of submarines at sea from two-thirds of the force to one-third, would be quite visible to the Russians and easily monitored by watching submarine activity at a small number of coastal ports.

A reduction of Russian strategic submarine alert rates has occurred as a result of economic strain on operations and maintenance. From a normal cold war rate of about 20 percent, the Russians now keep less than 5 percent—only one or two SSBNs—at sea. However, that alert level is augmented by keeping some subs in port on alert with short reaction times for launch.

The Americans and Russians could thus agree to a strict limit on the number of submarines at sea or on alert at pierside, reducing the number to a handful on each side. The United States could readily count the submarines at sea by taking the difference between total inventory and total in port. On-site inspections would be very helpful in ascertaining the alert status of submarines in port, however.

Major Dealerting Measures for Strategic Bombers

Russian, and formerly Soviet, heavy bombers with long-range strategic missions have always been maintained, except during crises, at a low level of combat readiness bereft of nuclear payloads. In contrast, the United States maintained a significant fraction (declining from 50 percent to 33 percent to 25 percent from the 1960s to the 1980s) of its strategic bombers in a rapid reaction posture. U.S. alert bombers were loaded with nuclear weapons and ready to takeoff within fifteen minutes of a launch order.

The United States adopted the low-key alert status of Soviet bombers in 1991 on orders from President Bush. This change, accompanied a broader

90   BRUCE G. BLAIR

reconfiguration of nuclear forces on both sides, not only reduced combat readiness but also strengthened Soviet control over weapons systems ranging from tactical nuclear weapons on ships to strategic rockets in silos.

Additional steps to dealert the bomber forces and extend the time necessary for their regeneration can be taken. The basic idea, which has many variations, is to relocate bomber payloads from their home bases to other storage locations far removed from the bombers themselves. The nuclear payloads no longer would be collocated with the delivery systems.

In one variant the payloads could be consolidated at storage depots at one or a very small number of military airstrips. The bombers would then have to fly to the airstrip to receive their nuclear arms. The flight time plus the loading time would be lengthy because of the inability of the depot and airstrip to handle many bombers at once. A long queue would develop that would delay loading, and once loaded the bombers would still have to return to their home base or fly to wartime dispersal bases.

A second variant is identical except that the consolidated storage depot for bomber payloads would not be located near a usable bomber airstrip. The payloads would be accessible only by ground vehicles—truck or rail— or possibly helicopters, which would deliver them to a distant airstrip for loading onto bombers. The extra time for ground travel would extend the period of regeneration substantially beyond that outlined in the first variant.

A third variation would entail the use of vacant missile silos (marked for destruction in the next several years if current plans go forward) to store the payloads. Three hundred Minuteman silos in South Dakota and Missouri have already been emptied, and another two hundred will be vacated before the end of the decade. Similar activity is under way in Russia. Instead of destroying these hardened silos as part of the START reduction of strategic warheads, the parties could agree to exempt them from START counting rules and allow their use for nuclear warhead storage as long as adequate arrangements for joint monitoring are instituted.[142] These arrangements would follow the outlines of the joint monitoring from field control posts described earlier.

142. A similar concept for using vacant missile silos to store plutonium cores from dismantled nuclear weapons under joint U.S.-Russian and International Atomic Energy Agency monitoring is discussed in Bruce G. Blair, "Securing and Storing Nuclear Materials and Waste: A Novel Mission for the Military" (Brookings, forthcoming).

The advantage of silo storage is that the payloads would be inaccessible to bombers and yet be afforded a very high degree of protection from attack. Their retrieval and delivery to bomber airstrips would require elaborate and time-consuming procedures, of course. And for cruise missile warheads in silos, an additional lengthy period would be needed to mate the warheads to the missiles. The cruise missiles themselves could be kept in storage at the primary bomber bases; the loading of the bombers would delay regeneration even more.

In all these variants the payloads would be placed under joint or multilateral monitoring to ensure advance warning of any move to regenerate strategic bombers. Additional confidence-building measures could be established to facilitate monitoring of the bombers themselves. For instance, prior notification would be given for any bomber flights to airstrips with bomber payload depots. Furthermore, the parties would exchange information on the location of the depots (or silos used for this purpose), and the distribution of payloads within the storage system to calibrate national technical means of verification as well as on-site portal monitoring.

Radical Dealerting Measures for ICBMs and SSBNs

More radical measures could be adopted to create a configuration of strategic forces in which their use on any scale, large or small, would require some readily detectable preparation that would take at least twenty-four hours to complete. The strategic postures ultimately should be modified so that these preparations would take weeks or months to complete. The monitoring arrangements would seek to ensure that any weapons brought to a state of readiness that allowed for their immediate use were transparent to others, so that a real or apparent breakout could not upset the strategic balance.

This is not to imply that the forces would necessarily depend for their survival on timely strategic warning of a potential adversary's breakout. A portion of the strategic forces could and should still be deployed in an inherently survivable mode so that no decisive advantage could accrue from cheating.

Putting aside all the international and domestic political resistance to a global zero-alert policy that would terminate the daily alert practices of both established and new nuclear states, the proposal clearly faces daunting obstacles. A major one is a lack of workable proposals on how to deploy the forces so that they cannot be employed quickly, and lend themselves to verification of that constraint, yet remain sufficiently survivable and reconstitutable that they could support a strategy of delayed retaliation.[143]

The dealerting option discussed for bombers, particularly the variant that would use empty missile silos to store payloads, appears to go a long way toward meeting the essential requirements of verification and, to a lesser extent, survivability. By contrast, the combination of ICBM detargeting and dealerting options discussed earlier only partially meets the strict criteria of zero alert for land-based strategic missiles. It partially satisfies the verification criterion and delays the regeneration of the full ICBM force for more than twenty-four hours. But the measures do not preclude the regeneration of some Russian and U.S. land-based missiles within a relatively short period. A small number of these missiles could be readied for launch in a few hours. Similarly, the detargeting and dealerting options proposed for submarines could virtually eliminate the potential for rapid launch, but the options are often not conducive to reliable and timely verification.

A better approach is to separate warheads from missiles. Properly designed, this separation would indisputably solve the problem of quick employment. But any such plsn would seem to increase the difficulties of protecting the components, particularly the warheads in storage, from attack. No one has put forward a design that ensures the invulnerability of the separated components under plausible breakout conditions, in spite of effective monitoring arrangements. The idea is not necessarily unsound for this reason; it is only that the burden of proof is heavy.

Conversely, no one has illustrated how intact forces (all components including warheads mated to the delivery systems), operating in a manner that preserves their invulnerability, could be verifiably deprived of quick launch readiness for twenty-four hours or longer.

Some crude solutions to the conundrum have been offered. Richard Garwin suggested putting mountains of gravel on the tops of ICBM silos. It would take days to clear away the gravel from any silo being prepared for launch, yet the missile inside would retain its protection from enemy

---

143. An early proposal for a strategy of delayed retaliation was elaborated in Bruce G. Blair, *Strategic Command and Control* (Brookings, 1985), especially pp. 289-95. Dubbed "no immediate second use," the proposal required nuclear retaliation to be delayed for at least twenty-four hours.

attack. The idea is ingenious, but it fails to solve the problem of how to protect the vulnerable bulldozers and their operators from attack. (It is also somewhat impractical to perform regular maintenance on missiles if their silos have to be cleared each time to get access.) A similiar problem pertains to retrieving bomber payloads from storage depots.

The options I now propose verifiably preclude the quick employment of sea- and land-based ballistic missiles while protecting the forces' capability for reconstitution and delayed employment. They validate the technical feasibility of zero alert. There is really little doubt that solutions can be found for any and all categories of strategic forces, including the hardest case, ballistic missile submarines.

REMOVING GUIDANCE SETS FROM SSBNS. The strategic submarine force seems the worst candidate for zero alert. The fleet consists of a relatively small number of vessels that depend heavily on stealth for their survival. They are easy targets in port, where they undergo time-consuming preparations for alert patrols. But on patrol they become totally self-reliant, eminently capable of launch, and immune to external observation. These characteristics, combined with the fact that installing warheads on submarine missiles is an elaborate operation that exposes SSBNs on the surface for a long time and renders them extremely vulnerable, make this launch platform a problematic case for zero alert.

A technically sound plan for submarine zero alert is not unimaginable, however. Such a plan would be especially important for U.S. submarines. First, they carry the bulk of U.S. strategic warheads and hence represent the cornerstone of America's deterrence strategy. A zero-alert plan that would preserve their invulnerability is essential to support a doctrine of delayed retaliation. Second, they pose a severe first-strike threat to Russia that zero alert would remove. The pinpoint accuracy of their D-5 missiles, potential for quick release, short flight times, and relative opaqueness to Russian warning sensors make them the bane of Russian strategic planners. More than any other strategic leg, U.S. sea-based missiles compel Russia to maintain a posture of launch on warning for the bulk of its ICBM force.

But consider the following zero-alert idea for U.S. strategic submarines. Suppose that the force would operate at sea in the regular fashion but with one critical difference: the submarines would leave port without guidance units for any of the missiles on board. The missiles (twenty-four in a Trident SSBN) would be partially disassembled and could not be launched without the missing guidance sets.

The critical missing components could be kept safely in storage on board attack submarines (SSNs) deployed at sea. Under routine practices, the components would remain separated at all times. In an emergency the two types of submarines could rendevous on orders from higher authority or according to a prearranged schedule that would go into effect were an attack to sever communications. To transfer the essential cargo—twenty-four missile guidance sets for each SSBN—each pair of subs would have to meet on the surface and haul the sets (each about the size of half an oil barrel) using light equipment from the storage compartment through the supply-personnel hatch of the attack submarine. The sets would be hauled to the strategic submarine and down to its storage area.

This transfer could be accomplished with a few hours of work on the surface without significant risk of detection. By contrast, a similiar concept involving the separation of warheads from the missiles would risk almost certain detection and would vastly increase the SSBNs vulnerability to attack because the two submarines would have to remain on the surface for several days. The mating of the warheads to the missiles would require the use of heavy equipment, notably cranes, and access to the missiles through the launch tubes. The transfer would be a delicate procedure that would be possible only on calm seas.

After completing the transfer of the guidance sets, the submarines could immediately submerge and the SSBN would begin the time-consuming task of installing the sets. The normal contingent of technicians assigned to a strategic submarine are trained to perform this task and often do so during alert patrols. A typical submarine carries two spare guidance sets to replace units found to be defective during the weapons system checkout performed in preparation for going on full combat alert.

The weapons technicians would need about three days to install all twenty-four units. One day after the rendevous and transfer, the SSBN could achieve a launch capability for eight missiles (or forty warheads under START II planning assumptions). Three hours after submerging, one missile with five warheads could be readied for launch. Although this fails to meet the criterion of zero alert, other operational constraints could be imposed to ensure that no missile could be prepared for immediate use without giving reliable warning that the preparations were under way.

Besides exchanging specific information on the inventory and disposition of guidance sets, the key monitoring arrangements would rely on separating the at-sea SSBNs and SSNs by large distances and on conducting physical or electronic inspections of both types. Submarines in port, and the warheads for them, would be subject to on-site inspection by joint monitoring teams.

Patrol areas off limits to SSNs would be demarcated for the SSBNs. The attack susbmarines would be prohibited from operating in waters anywhere close to the strategic sub patrol area. More specifically, the distance separating the SSNs and the closest boundary of the SSBN patrol areas would always exceed the closing mileage the two submarines could log in twenty-four hours (about 1,700 nautical miles).

SSNs could operate in waters close to the coasts and make numerous port calls to lend visibility to the operation. At any time, they could be instructed to surface, report their location, and submit to inspection by monitoring teams at a nearby port. These challenges could be made for only one SSN at a time (several others would be at sea at any time in support of the five strategic submarines on alert (based on a reduced alert rate for the fourteen Tridents planned for deployment).

For their part the SSBNs would periodically confirm their adherence to limitations on combat patrol zones and their lack of guidance sets. They could do so by following either of two procedures. In one, regions within the boundaries of the agreed patrol zone would be designated for situating surface ships with joint or multinational monitoring crews. These ships would carry no weapons or technical means for detecting submerged submarines. The Tridents submitting to verification would periodically approach the ships and surface. The monitoring ships would identify the sub and either board it to confirm the absence of guidance sets or receive electronic confirmation from special seals on the missiles that would be broken if guidance sets had been installed. (This provision deals with the possibility that vessels other than SSNs, or aircraft, might secretly deliver the guidance sets to the SSBNs.) These seals would have been developed by Russia and equipped for transmitting codes known only by Russia. (At some point this function could be assumed by international monitoring bodies.) Visual and instrumental inspection carried out during their original placement on the SSBN would ensure that the equipment does not carry any explosive agents or any other devices that could be exploited to compromise the plan.

Information on the contact, including the SSBN identification, would then be transmitted to the Russians and Americans. The schedule of contacts would be determined so that, on the one hand, it would exclude the possibility of simultaneously locating more than one Trident on patrol while on the other hand ensuring that no SSBN moves outside the permitted zone during the interval between contacts.

The second procedure would be the same except that the coded information from the SSBN would be delivered to the monitoring ships by means of a radio buoy. If the released buoy were timed to transmit the coded signals after a delay of, say, one hour, the submarine could preserve its stealth and invulnerability while adhering to monitoring rules.

Assuming that the Russian strategic submarine force has a comparable technical configuration, the same strictures would apply to it and its SSN support operations. The effect of these rules on Russian sea-based strategic operations would not be nearly as dramatic as it would be on American SSBN operations, however, because of the historically low tempo of at-sea alert activity by the Russian submarines.

This asymmetrical impact should not be judged in isolation from other strategic operations, however. The zero-alert plan discussed next would have a much larger impact on Russian than on American land-based strategic forces.

REMOVING CRITICAL COMPONENTS FROM ICBMS. Zero alert for the ICBM forces could be instituted by removing warheads or guidance sets from the missiles. Another critical component for silo-based ICBMs is a collimator, the removal of which from a silo would disable the missile's guidance.

The most stringent dealerting measure for land-based missiles would be to remove their warheads and place them in storage under joint or multilateral monitoring. Warheads would be retrieved from depots and mated to missiles only under emergency conditions that threaten national security and necessitate a nuclear option requiring ICBMs.

The Soviet Union actually adopted such a procedure for its early generations of ICBM forces, a reflection of its emphasis on nuclear safeguards and its confidence in obtaining timely warning of an enemy strike. During most of the 1960s the Soviets refrained, except for brief periods during crises, from mating warheads to land-based strategic rockets, intermediate-range ballistic missiles (IRBMs) and medium-range ballistic missiles (MRBMs) as well as ICBMs.[144] Warheads were kept in bunkers miles to tens of miles from the launch pads. A special unit of the Defense Ministry and the general staff, separate from the commanders of

---

144. This paragraph draws on Blair, *Logic of Accidental Nuclear War.*

the strategic rockets, maintained and guarded the warheads. In an emergency requiring preparation of the rockets, the special unit would have received orders through its own separate chain of command and would have delivered the warheads to the launch pads and mated them to the rockets.

The philosophy underlying zero alert and the specific proposal for removing warheads from missiles are thus compatible with early Soviet practice. In contrast, from the beginning of the nuclear missile age the United States stressed the need for rapid reaction with warheads mated to launch-ready missiles even in peacetime. This tradition reflected a fear of intelligence failure and belief in the plausibility of a surprise Soviet attack.

The Soviet Union eventually abandoned its earlier practices and adopted a rapid reaction posture similar to the U.S. posture. Both geared their command systems and wartime procedures for launch on warning, committing fixed-based (silo) ICBMs in particular to quick launch. The Soviets went so far as to configure mobile ICBMs as well as pierside submarines for fast launch.

Getting the two strategic cultures to abandon this commitment may be the greatest challenge to proponents of zero alert. Russia particularly might resist separating warheads from ICBMs because the bulk of its strategic arsenal is carried by ICBMs. The Russian strategic rocket forces have always been the premier service in the armed forces and the backbone of the country's strategic deterrent.

The START II Treaty works to nearly equalize the role of ICBMs in each side's overall arsenal. For the United States, ICBMs will represent about 14 percent of the 3,500 warhead allotment allowed by START. On the Russian side, ICBMs will drop to a historical low of 20 to 25 percent of the total deployment of warheads. Mobile truck-based ICBMs, the single-warhead SS-25s, will be the centerpiece of the Russian ICBM force. Russia plans to deploy 500 to 600 mobile SS-25s. In addition, several hundred SS-25s and SS-19s with single warheads will be placed in silos.

Russia would keenly feel the effect of separating warheads from ICBMs because of low peacetime readiness levels and the relative vulnerability of its strategic bombers and submarines. If Russia would remove warheads from ICBMs, it could not fall back on other legs for nearly as much support as the United States would get from its, particularly from SSBNs. In consequence, Russia must be assured that its ICBM force would not become vulnerable under zero alert, that its resilience would be preserved just as the U.S. SSBNs preserve their invulnerability under the zero-alert plan outlined earlier.

The mobile SS-25 missiles are Russia's mainstay in providing this assurance. In peacetime a regiment or battalion out of each SS-25 division regularly operates out of garrison. This practice, which protects the forces in the field from direct attack, could continue under a zero-alert regime for ICBMs. The units in the field and those in garrison would have to submit to periodic inspection, however, to ensure that warheads had not been installed.

Joint monitoring stations at the SS-25 main base would check out the status of units returning to garrison from the field, and inspectors would routinely verify that missiles in garrison lacked warheads. Units operating for extended periods in the field would have to report to the monitoring stations for periodic inspection.

The warheads for the mobile SS-25 missiles would have to be removed from the area of field deployment to another region of the country. They could be placed in storage facilities, even vacant missile silos, or in mobile depots such as specially equipped trains or trucks. A mobile storage system should be able to provide adequate protection for the warheads. Russia has an extensive grid of railway lines and experience operating strategic weapons on trainborne platforms; it deploys, for instance, a trainborne force of SS-24 ICBMs. It could take advantage of this rail infrastructure and experience with exploiting rail mobility for strategic protection in managing the warhead stocks for the SS-25 missiles deployed a considerable distance away. Moscow surely could devise an ingenious concept of operations that would enable the warheads to rendezvous with mobile missiles, mate, and reconstitute a retaliatory capability in the event of U.S. strategic reconstitution and sudden attack.

U.S.-Russian inspection teams would periodically take inventory of the stockpiles. Trains or trucks carrying the warheads would at regular intervals show up at designated monitoring stations and submit to inventory control. Warheads at fixed locations would be routinely visited and counted.

Warheads and missiles normally housed in silos would also be separated by large distances and monitored. The missiles would be periodically inspected by joint monitoring teams based at division-level rocket bases in Russia and wing-level missile bases in the United States. Those warheads consolidated at storage depots in both countries could be continuously watched by on-site joint monitoring teams. Part or all of the Russian warheads might be handled in the same manner as warheads for mobile missiles and subjected to the same monitoring arrangements. The United States doubtless would not opt for using trains or other mobile platforms to store its warheads.

One of the major drawbacks of separating warheads from U.S. missiles is that the capacity of the support infrastructure is so limited that the emergency reconstitution of the ICBM force would take years to complete. The air force could load Minuteman III warheads only at a snail's pace because of limited transport equipment, warhead bays, installation equipment, and trained crews. A substantial investment would be required to eliminate the logistics shortcoming.

This drawback also applies to the reinstallation of guidance sets removed from Minuteman III missiles. The effect of taking guidance sets from the missiles would be nearly the same as for removing warheads. The launch readiness of the ICBM force would be comparably reduced by either measure. Similarly, equipment shortages mean that reinstalling guidance sets in an emergency would stretch out over years. Such lengthy preparations, even if substantially shortened, would doubtless exceed the tolerance of U.S. strategic planners.

An alternative to removing warheads or guidance systems from silo-based missiles, American or Russian, would be to misalign the guidance systems and take out critical pieces of hardware from the silo equipment room. To prepare missiles for combat, collimator equipment used to align and calibrate the missile's guidance system by means of light beams would have to be brought into each silo. Missile realignment would be a time-consuming operation. The equipment is very sensitive and requires finesse and patience to fine-tune.

The procedures take far less time to perform than the alternatives, however. In an emergency the air force could reinstate proper guidance alignment for 500 Minuteman III missiles in a matter of weeks. This schedule would meet the time criteria of zero alert, and its visibility to monitors would largely satisfy the need for verification. Some supplementary monitoring arrangements involving on-site spot inspections would be necessary to remove any residual doubt.

Peacetime and Crisis Stability

Any zero-alert procedure must pass a test of peacetime and crisis stability. The first part of the test is simple: does the plan remove the ability of potential adversaries to mount a decisive sudden attack in peacetime? The second part is more complex. The postures must provide for transitional stability during the regeneration of nuclear forces in an emergency and ensure that the process bringing forces to peak readiness culminates in a stable balance between them.

It is important to recognize that another type of stability is at stake: safe and stringent control over nuclear weapons during peacetime and crisis redeployment. This stability is of course the whole point of zero alert in peacetime, and it follows that putting nuclear forces on alert during a crisis inevitably erodes it. A case could even be made that the virtues of zero alert in peacetime might be outweighed by its liabilities during crises, insofar as rusty organizations, forced to move from zero to full alert without the benefit of recent experience in mating warheads to missiles and generally managing high levels of combat readiness, would be more prone to errors and accidents.

The best rebuttal to this argument is that zero alert would strongly militate against large-scale strategic reconstitution in the first place. First it would inhibit the initial escalation of alert levels during a crisis. Second, the experience presently gained by daily alert operations, if greater than under zero alert, still falls well short of the experience necessary to manage alert operations safely during a crisis. The standards of safety that have evolved through repetitive, experiential learning during thirty-five years of aggressive alert operations have not been extended to the circumstances of advanced crisis or to the actual initiation of combat operations. There is scant reason to believe that past experience would enable organizations to cope well with the stress and unpredictability of an intense nuclear crisis. No organization has demonstrated an ability to adapt under these circumstances.

PEACETIME STABILITY. In removing all warheads or other vital components from delivery systems and adopting other measures of zero alert, the nuclear superpowers would heavily discount the plausibility of a bolt from the blue and embrace the principle of safety first. Yet prudent planners need reassurance that the configuration of strategic forces under zero alert is completely stable, that is, the strategic balance is insensitive to a sudden change of a potential adversary's intentions.

Such reassurance could derive from the certainty that zero alert precludes the quick firing of any strategic weapons, or at least prevents a potential adversary from firing sufficient numbers to gain a decisive advantage. This confidence depends on properly designing the dealerting measures, full mutual disclosure and acceptance of the steps to be taken, and comprehensive monitoring to ensure that the complete plan is carried out.[145]

Reassurance could also be derived from designing the measures to ensure that sufficient friendly forces are inherently invulnerable. This hedging principle applies in the case of U.S. SSBNs based at sea with their vital missile guidance sets carried by SSNs also based at sea. Even in the unlikely event of a critical flaw in the zero-alert plan that would enable Russia to launch a sudden nuclear strike, the United States would retain a secure and formidable retaliatory force. Assuming the zero-alert options for SSBNs discussed earlier—cutting back the at-sea alert rate to 5 Trident submarines—were adopted, the surviving force could still generate 600 warheads (after START II reductions to five warheads a missile). That is an ample hedge in light of the severe limits imposed on Russian forces under a zero-alert agreement.[146]

On the Russian side, the hedging principle would apply to mobile SS-25 ICBMs dispersed in the field with their warheads carried by trains and trucks also dispersed in the field. Such a plan handles the pessimistic scenario of a sudden attack by U.S. forces exploiting a loophole in the overall zero-alert plan. The size of the survivable Russian arsenal would

145. For a thoughtful elaboration of this theme, see Jonathan Dean, "The Final Stage of Nuclear Arms Control," PRAC paper no. 10, University of Maryland, Center for International and Security Studies, August 1994.

146. A number of leading experts have advocated smaller allowable arsenals. One thorough study recommends a limit of 200 deployed warheads on each side with no more than 25 warheads on alert at any one time. Ivo H. Daalder, "Stepping Down the Thermonuclear Ladder: How Low Can We Go?" in Ivo H. Daalder and Terry Terriff, eds., *Rethinking the Unthinkable: New Directions for Nuclear Arms Control* (London: Frank Cass, 1993). Jonathan Dean also calls for a ceiling of 200 warheads on the arsenals of every nuclear state but proposes that they be separated from their delivery systems and placed under international monitoring. See "Final Stage of Nuclear Arms Control." The radical proposal of global nuclear disarmament is advanced in a visionary article by Barry M. Blechman and Cathleen S. Fisher, "Phase Out the Bomb," *Foreign Policy*, no. 97 (Winter 1994-95), pp. 79-95.

be comparable to the U.S. arsenal of survivable forces if the Russians were to deploy 500 to 600 single-warhead SS-25s and either keep a large fraction of them in the field or ready for quick dispersal out of garrison on tactical warning. The most practical stance would keep one regiment out of each division (a third or less of the force) in the field at any given time. Between 150 and 200 missiles would constantly be untargetable, depending on the total number of SS-25s the Russians would finally deploy. Compared with the United States, the number of survivable Russian warheads would be smaller in peacetime, but their total explosive yield would be just as large.[147]

TRANSITIONAL STABILITY. Scenarios requiring, or seeming to recommend, the regeneration of nuclear capability mostly strain credulity, but should circumstances call for preparing a nuclear option, the act of reconstitution should allow for transitional stability. This stability depends on timely notification or warning of the change in posture, on preventing any spontaneous escalation of alert levels, and on taking counterbalancing responses designed to deny a potential adversary any decisive preemptive advantage it might otherwise obtain by changing its nuclear posture.

Among the scenarios that might recommend or require a departure from zero alert, the following discussion treats four, beginning with the most plausible.

The most likely circumstance is perhaps one in which the United States would generate a nuclear option to deal with a third world contingency, such as a nuclear threat from North Korea to U.S. forces deployed in South Korea. In such a case, any U.S. nuclear strike plan would involve very small numbers of U.S. weapons. The strategic command or a theater commander would likely draw up a plan whose nuclear component would more likely feature tactical than strategic weapons. But the strategic command could also devise limited attack options or selected attack options that would employ strategic forces against the adversary.

Regardless of the type and scale of the planned operation, however, the general rule to be followed would be that the party breaking out of the

---

147. Most U.S. SSBN warheads have yields of 100 kilotons each, although a substantial fraction will be D-5 warheads with 300 to 450 kilotons. Russian SS-25s carry warheads with an estimated yield of 750 kilotons. The aggregate destructive power of the survivable arsenals on each side is virtually equivalent.

zero-alert posture would notify the other parties of its intentions, identify the pertinent weapons systems to be redeployed for combat, and clarify the alerting steps and combat actions to be taken. This norm could be strengthened by designating a special storage area from which a small number of weapons could be returned to alert if that ever proved to be necessary. The limited number would provide reassurance that a larger regeneration was not being screened by the smaller contingency. This arrangement, coupled with joint monitoring already in place and national technical means of verification, should provide ample reassurance to the other parties to a zero-alert agreement in cases of very small operations. Preparation of a small nuclear option to deal with third world contingencies should not trigger uncontrolled escalatory interaction between the major nuclear powers nor warrant any significant compensatory response by the onlooking power.

The most plausible scenario pitting the major nuclear powers against each other and possibly recommending raising the level of nuclear alert above zero features turmoil in the former Soviet Union. Political incoherence in Moscow or an outbreak of hostilities between Russia and Ukraine, either of which could degrade the cohesion of Russian nuclear command and control and project a greater nuclear threat at the United States, might seem to warrant a precautionary U.S. nuclear alert involving extensive redeployment of strategic forces.

But the regeneration of strategic capability could well be an inappropriate response. If Russian nuclear control convulses under internal pressures, the Western response should, at least initially, be to provide reassurance and even assistance, even though the situation might increase the nuclear threat to the West. The real danger would be inadvertent launch, not deliberate attack, and nuclear restraint would be more constructive than aggressive alert responses. Raising the alert level of U.S. forces to increase deterrence could initiate reciprocal escalation of alert levels as well as make it more difficult for the Russian command system to restore strict control over its own nuclear forces.

One of the important features of zero alert is of course that it reduces, in the first instance, the chances and consequences of Russia's losing control over its nuclear weapons. Zero alert serves as a buffer against contingencies that pose far greater danger when nuclear forces are kept on launch-ready alert. Furthermore, zero alert requires that the command systems take a major discontinuous step to regenerate strategic capability.

This vastly increases the likelihood that nuclear alerting would be a considered act of national policy. Crisis alerting becomes less the diffuse process it presently is, with less chance that incremental steps could be taken by a decentralized command system driven by military exigencies. Under zero alert the threshold would be raised to such heights that only a deliberate decision by top civilian authority could cross it. This strengthens top-level control over the process and inhibits spontaneous escalation.

A less likely scenario involving the major nuclear powers as principals is a resumption of relations reminiscent of the cold war to which they respond by raising the alert level above zero for some nuclear forces. Although ill-advised from the standpoint of safety, a more aggressive alert policy might seem warranted if relations between the superpowers deteriorated.

Starting from a base line of zero alert, the steps taken to raise alert levels could be measured and adopted cautiously to avoid triggering an uncontrolled spiral in combat readiness. Regeneration should remain under the firm control of national authorities, who would be well advised to notify their opposites of any alerting steps in store. These steps could be discrete, proportionate to the opposing side's moves, and regulated by prior agreement. Presumably there would be protocols to define and limit this process in advance should it ever be deemed necessary. Such protocols, coupled with in-place monitoring arrangements and independent means of surveillance, would provide reassurance that the alert responses on each side would not destabilize the strategic balance. Transitional stability should hold.

The least likely scenario engaging the major powers in escalatory alert features a classic confrontation with one side anticipating a conflict that might involve military hostilities and deciding to break out of a zero-alert posture. One or both powers could annul their cooperative partnership and dissolve the zero-alert agreement, and an uncontrolled escalatory spiral could ensue. All parties would then receive unambiguous warning from joint monitoring teams and other sources that large-scale preparations were under way. The escalation of alert readiness would become mutually reinforcing as nuclear forces were brought as quickly as possible to maximum wartime readiness.

The chances are remote that this scenario would develop without first passing through a phase in which a deterioration of relations between the nuclear superpowers would lead to a gradual heightening of the alert level for some forces. This precursor scenario could have the effect of moderating the transitional instability that accompanies the subsequent crisis scenario because additional forces on both sides had already adopted a stable alert configuration before the all-out race began. The opportunity to gain a decisive advantage by abandoning all restraint would be smaller.

Breaking out of a partial or complete zero alert should not even confer a significant advantage. The monitoring arrangements would provide timely warning, allowing all parties to respond with balancing measures. If all the zero-alert options presented earlier were adopted by both sides, neither the United States nor Russia could rapidly regenerate their forces, and they could do so only at roughly equivalent speed.

Even if alerting responses were unduly delayed on one side for political or military reasons, transitional instability would be moderated by the sizable number of inherently invulnerable strategic forces maintained by both sides at all times under zero alert. As noted earlier, this includes 600 survivable and potentially deliverable U.S. SLBM warheads at sea.

Along the crucial dimension of safety, however, this type of crisis would threaten transitional stability. Combat readiness would take precedence over safety for the sake of projecting a greater nuclear threat at a potential aggressor. Warheads would be mated to delivery vehicles and the command systems could revert to their cold war predilection for rapid reaction or literal launch on warning even if they had been redesigned to support delayed retaliation. In consequence the risks of accidental, unauthorized, or inadvertent use of nuclear weapons would rise.

END-STATE STABILITY. End-state stability has one basic component. Having reached a state of maximum combat readiness, the command systems should be able to support a strategy of delayed retaliation. This means that the established wartime mission of the nuclear forces could be accomplished without resort to launch on warning or launch under attack.

The U.S. strategic nuclear forces have never been able to meet this requirement. For decades they have been saddled with ensuring that a huge number of all types of enemy targets—nuclear forces, other military targets, leadership, and war-supporting industry—would be destroyed in wartime. This national directive made rapid reaction crucially important to achieving the required level of damage expectancy, especially damage to the Soviet nuclear forces. The U.S. command system set itself on a hair trigger to ensure comprehensive target coverage. The Russian system for its own reasons followed suit.

Under START and the zero-alert options outlined earlier, the U.S. strategic forces could adopt a strategy of delayed retaliation that meets reasonable criteria for target coverage—enough to project a credible wartime threat of retaliation sufficient to deter a potential adversary even under conditions of intense nuclear crisis. The criteria are that U.S. strategic forces at peak readiness provide for 66 percent damage expectancy against 1,000 targets in the following categories: nuclear forces (450 targets, including 350 silos and 100 nuclear support facilities);[148] other military targets (200 targets); leadership and nuclear command and control (100 targets); and war-supporting industry (250 targets).[149] In addition, the strategic forces have to retain a reserve of 100 deliverable warheads.

These requirements translate into a force structure consisting of 950 survivable warheads under enduring command and control.[150] As noted earlier, the zero-alert U.S. SSBN force (five at-sea Tridents) alone would carry 600 survivable warheads, or about 60 percent of the total needed. There is no doubt that the balance could be generated if necessary in a crisis. Putting an additional three SSBNs carrying 360 warheads on alert would suffice to ensure comprehensive target coverage. These enduring

148. The Russians might deploy fewer ICBMs in silos, but they are not expected to deploy more than this number. A case can be made for dropping the requirement to target individual silos in favor of targeting only the launch control centers and local division support infrastructure. This approach would threaten to severely disrupt the continuity of ICBM operations while expending a small part of the warheads needed to attack silos.

149. The core target sets in this category include 72 Russian military final assembly plants (17 missile, 16 aircraft, 14 electronics, 13 shipbuilding, 12 tanks and other land arms); 13 Russian nuclear production facilities; 11 chemical or biological production facilities; and 40 major component producers. The locations of these 150 facilities are shown in Central Intelligence Agency, *The Defense Industries of the Newly Independent States of Eurasia*, OSE 93-10001 (January 1993).

150. This assumes a launch reliability and warhead penetration rate of 80 percent. The target coverage goal requires 660 deliverable weapons on targets plus 100 deliverable reserve warheads. To compensate for a 20 percent rate of unreliability, 950 survivable warheads would be needed.

forces would not have to be launched quickly in the event of war if the United States had designed a resilient command and communications network to support them.

The example above clearly suggests that if all U.S. and Russian strategic weapons allowed by START II were brought to alert under crisis conditions, the stability of the end state would be high from at least a U.S. perspective. The United States would in fact need to generate only a portion of its arsenal (perhaps three Trident submarines in addition to the five normally at sea) to satisfy target requirements and support delayed retaliation. Twelve Trident submarines in fact would easily support a zero-alert posture with five always at sea and three seaworthy in port.[151] The remainder of the U.S. strategic forces are surplus forces from the standpoint of central deterrence. The potential role of the leftover forces in supporting other missions involving third world contingencies may or may not prove compelling enough to justify their retention in significant numbers. The vast majority could retired without risk.

Conclusion

Safety is not now the primary goal of nuclear security policy, but a wiser policy would make it so. That safety should become the primary commitment is justified by the favorable climate of U.S.-Russian relations, the easing of the requirements of deterrence among the charter nuclear states, the difficulties of nuclear control in the former Soviet Union resulting from political turbulence and economic duress, and the emergence of nuclear states with fledgling and unproven systems of command and control.

An effective and realistic remedy for the gamut of safety problems that plague all the nuclear states would be to take all nuclear weapons off alert, remove warheads or other vital components from the delivery systems, and institute international monitoring arrangements to verify adherence to a zero-alert agreement. Serious study of various options for lowering the readiness of nuclear forces and creating an international taboo against hair-trigger nuclear postures should be undertaken.

We should strive to further lengthen the fuse on all nuclear forces, extending the time needed to bring them to launch-ready status to weeks,

---

151. Two submarines normally would be undergoing overhaul at any given time.

months, and ultimately years. This is not as far-fetched technically as it may seem. For example, if all warheads were removed from Minuteman missiles, the air force estimates that it would require more than four years working at breakneck speed under emergency conditions to reinstall 3 warheads on each of the 500 missiles deployed under START II. That is virtually as long as the United States took to mobilize the Manhattan project and build a nuclear bomb from scratch during World War II. We cannot stuff the nuclear genie much more firmly into the bottle than that. In effect, such a zero-alert plan is tantamount to nuclear disarmament. In any case, the exact accounting and internationalized monitoring required to establish zero alert is almost certainly a necessary condition for the eventual elimination of nuclear arsenals, and projecting their eventual elimination is very likely to be a necessary condition for effectively managing the general process of weapons proliferation.[152]

The principle of safety and the enabling arrangements ought to be the core themes of new, top-level political guidance and the key items on the agenda of future nuclear negotiations among the declared nuclear states. This redirection of nuclear policy would not only squarely face the danger of nuclear anarchy and inadvertent war, but would seek to eliminate the ability of any state to launch a sudden nuclear attack. Zero alert can accomplish both aims. It would also downgrade the importance of nuclear weapons in international affairs, demonstrate a serious commitment to the disarmament obligation enjoined by the Nuclear Non-Proliferation Treaty, and exert pressures on the undeclared nuclear states to follow suit. Not least, zero alert would be tangible proof of the end of the cold war.

152. I am indebted to John Steinbruner for this point.